CLASSIC RECIPES
·from·
CLASSIC fM

MICHAEL BARRY
with
KAROLYN SHINDLER

JARROLD

CLASSIC RECIPES FROM CLASSIC FM

Designed and produced by
Parke Sutton Publishing Limited, Norwich
for Jarrold Publishing, Norwich

Recipes by Michael Barry
Compiled by Karolyn Shindler
Food for photography by
The Banham Bakehouse, Norfolk
Food styling by Lesley de Boos
Photography by Andrew Perkins
Designed by Gillian Matthews
Edited by Anne Priestley

Text copyright © Michael Barry 1993
This edition © Jarrold Publishing 1993

ISBN 0-7117-0662-X

Printed in England

CONTENTS

INTRODUCTION

I do enjoy cooking on the radio. Not only can no one see when the milk boils over, but also there is a degree of direct communication that not even television can provide. There's another advantage too, and that's one for the listener. You can be given an idea for something to cook, shoot out to buy the ingredients, and come home to cook it for supper that day. What's more, you can get all the information you need and write it down without having to watch or read anything. There is one major disadvantage, of course. When the recipe starts, it's often not possible to write it down. The telephone rings, you're in the car, the pen has run out, or any one of 101 other excitements intervenes. And that's where this book comes in. In it are written down the most successful recipes we have broadcast during the Henry Kelly show on Classic FM over the last year. They are broadcast every morning just after 10.30 and attract one of the largest audiences on the station.

Classic FM is essentially a music radio station – a classical music station – so the recipes have had to be both brief and classic in their own right. I have also tried to make them Crafty. Crafty cooking has been my speciality for 20 years and my golden rule is that if the food tastes delicious, looks wonderful and is easy to prepare, everybody is pleased. If there is a short-cut I take it, on condition it doesn't affect the taste of the dish. I've included some Crafty hints and tips as well, gathered specially to make it easier for you to cook great meals for your family and friends. They include the incredible Crafty white sauce, a Crafty way of cooking pasta, and hints on how to get the best out of new potatoes; all part and parcel of the ideas and advice you will find in the book.

Ingredients are very important to me as well. I think careful shopping is not only fun but also takes half the work out of cooking. I use fresh ingredients where possible and always the best there are, of whatever food I am buying. Alpine Salt is one of these. Pure salt supplied in three different forms – plain, with herbs, and reduced sodium – is an essential part of many of the dishes in this book. The recipes have been written down and annotated by Karolyn Shindler, without whose contribution, I must say, the book would probably not exist. They are divided into easy-to-use sections, from soups and starters through to the 'puddins' that are the feature of the spot every Friday. I hope you'll find there's a wide variety within the sections from cheap 'n cheerful to grand dinner party recipes, and from quick puddings to the most popular recipe we have ever broadcast on the station, The Ultimate Chocolate Cake. This is a rich, dark, moist confection, effortless to make and not to be missed.

I hope you enjoy this collection of Classic FM recipes. Not just an entertainment or even an appetiser but an easy-to-use guide to delicious dining and, not least, to some healthy eating.

THE CRAFTY COOK'S INFALLIBLE HINTS FOR MAKING IT EASY AND GETTING IT RIGHT

THE RIGHT TOOLS

GOOD QUALITY NON-STICK SAUCEPANS AND FRYING PANS will revolutionise your washing up and should affect your waistline – you will not need so much fat or oil for frying. There is an enormous range available – spend a bit more now and you will be happily using them in 10 years.

BUY THE RIGHT COOKING SPOONS, SLICES, ETC – to go with the non-stick cookware.

BUY AT LEAST A LIQUIDISER. Better still is a liquidiser and a food processor.

LETTING THE SHOP DO IT FOR YOU

Some ingredients are just as good bought ready-prepared, and save you time.

PASSATA, a smooth Italian tomato purée, more liquid than the stuff that comes in jars or tubes which is really more of a concentrated paste. *Passata* is wonderful for soups and sauces and is not that expensive. You can buy it in jars of about half a litre (just under a pint), or in tetrapacks which are even cheaper.

FRESHLY SQUEEZED ORANGE JUICE. Unless you specifically want the fleshy bits left after squeezing, it is often cheaper to buy it from a supermarket, certainly quicker, and there is no mess!

TINNED TOMATOES WITH ADDED HERBS, and PESTO SAUCE (made from basil, pine nuts and olive oil).

PIECES OF CHICKEN, e.g. boned chicken breasts.

FROZEN LEAF SPINACH is an easy and very acceptable alternative to the fresh stuff in dishes like pies and quiches.

PASTRY, both fresh and frozen, are generally excellent.

WHEN IT IS BETTER TO DO IT YOURSELF

Fresh Parmesan cheese in a lump keeps in the fridge for weeks. Grate it just before serving; the difference is extraordinary.

COOKING PASTA

I discovered this method for hard pasta on the back of a pasta packet in Clapham in 1974 and have used it ever since.

Put a large saucepan of water on to boil and add a pinch of salt and a little olive oil. When it is boiling, put in the pasta and leave to boil for 3 minutes. Take it off the heat, put on the lid, and leave for 7 minutes. At the end of that time it will be perfectly cooked: not sticky but *al dente*.

THE CRAFTY WHITE SAUCE

This really does work a treat. It is easy, quick and infallible! Once made, you then add whatever flavouring the recipe needs.

INGREDIENTS

½ pt (300 ml) milk (full-fat or semi-skimmed – NOT skimmed)
1½ oz (40 g) cornflour
1 oz (25 g) butter
Alpine Salt and pepper
Pinch grated nutmeg – optional

METHOD

Put the milk, cornflour, butter, seasoning and nutmeg into the saucepan, whisk, place on the heat, whisk again 2 or 3 times – not continuously – as it heats through. As the mixture comes to the boil, give it a really thorough whisk. You will have produced a wonderfully glossy white sauce without any effort – or lumps!

HEATING BUTTER

Heat oil in a frying pan first before you add butter – it stops the butter burning.

When the recipe requires butter only, use your ears! The moment the butter stops hissing, put in whatever you are cooking. If you delay, the butter will be brown and you will have to start all over again.

HEATING CREAM, FROMAGE FRAIS, YOGHURT, ETC.

It helps to know what you can boil and what you must not.

CREAM will not curdle, separate or do anything nasty when it is heated. You can even boil it.

FOR THE LOW-FAT ALTERNATIVES, 1 teaspoon of cornflour added to each 5 fl oz (50 ml – i.e. a small pot) and beaten in, means you can simmer them without curdling, but do not fast boil them.

BARBECUES

To save burnt fingers and to keep the food in one piece when barbecueing, a fish-shaped grid with a long handle is invaluable. They are available from good kitchen, d-i-y or hardware shops.

ONIONS

Use Spanish onions whenever possible – they are quicker to peel and deal with.

NEW POTATOES

The very best new potatoes are, in season, Jersey Royals. Don't scrub them completely – just get off the dirt and the dark bits. This ensures you get both maximum flavour and retain most of the nutritional goodies which are in and just under the skin. You can clean them with a scrubbing brush, or what in our household is known as the green scrubby thing – a sort of cloth which you wrap round one palm, roll the potato against it and 5 seconds later the potato is clean! Before you cook them, make sure they are all the same size – cut any big potatoes in half. And always cook them in cold water with a big pinch of salt – don't

be tempted to put them into hot water to speed up the process. When cooked, drain them, and let them stand for just 5 seconds to let the steam off. Put them back into the hot, dry saucepan, add a knob of butter and some fresh mint. Roll them round and give them a minute to absorb the butter. Delicious!

SALAD

For a fresher salad, tear the salad leaves into pieces about half the size of a postcard. Never cut lettuce; this allows all the liquid to drain out and you are left with a soft and floppy salad. As you tear the leaves, you crush the veins closed and the liquid stays in the leaves. Wash the pieces thoroughly, put in a clean tea-towel to dry, then make the salad. Half an hour in the fridge after this makes it even crisper.

DE-SKINNING SOFT FRUITS

To remove skins from soft fruits like peaches or tomatoes, dip them in boiling water for 30 seconds, drain, and the skins slip off effortlessly.

QUICK WEIGHTS AND MEASURES

Instead of fiddling around trying to weigh 1 oz (25 g) of something, use a tablespoon. One slightly rounded tablespoon = 1 oz. And 5 fl oz (150 ml) can be measured in a small yoghurt or cream pot.

EASY-REFERENCE OVEN TEMPERATURES

Hot: gas mark 7 / 425°F / 210°C / 190°C fan-assisted oven, or the top of an Aga roasting oven.
Pretty hot: gas mark 5 / 375°F / 190°C / 170°C fan-assisted oven, or the bottom of an Aga roasting oven.
Medium: gas mark 4 / 350°F / 180°C / 160°C fan-assisted oven, or the bottom of an Aga roasting oven.
Low/cool: gas mark 2 / 300°F / 150°C / 140°C fan-assisted oven, or the top of an Aga simmering oven.

STARTERS

GAZPACHO
SERVES FOUR

This soup is quick to make and very fresh. I particularly like the bowls of little bits that accompany it – wonderfully crunchy with the rich garlicky taste of the soup.

INGREDIENTS

1 Spanish onion
$\frac{1}{2}$ cucumber
4 spring onions
2 cloves garlic
1 red pepper and 1 green pepper, de-seeded
8 ripe tomatoes, skinned
$\frac{1}{2}$ pt (300 ml) water + ice-cubes
1 pt (600 ml) tomato juice
2 tablespoons red wine vinegar
4 tablespoons olive oil
2 slices of bread

METHOD

To make the croutons, cut the bread into cubes and fry in 2 tablespoons of the olive oil until they are pale gold. Put them in a small bowl. Take the spring onions (which you have washed and trimmed), cut a chunk off the cucumber, and about a quarter off the red and green peppers. Dice them and put them into separate bowls. Trim and peel everything that needs it, and cut the Spanish onion, remaining cucumber, green and red peppers, spring onions and tomatoes into chunks. Put them with the tomato juice, the garlic, the rest of the olive oil, the wine vinegar, the water (but not the ice-cubes) into the blender, food processor or mixer, and give them a quick whizz. The mixture should not turn into a complete purée – the vegetables need still to have a slight texture. The soup will be a deep red with flecks of green and gold in it from the vegetables. If it needs seasoning, do it now. To serve, pour it into a big bowl so each person can take a couple of ladles of the soup and sprinkle on a pinch of all the goodies that you have chopped up and put into separate bowls. If you want to make it really cold, add a couple of ice-cubes to each serving. It is wonderfully rich and sharp, but not at all acidy.

Gazpacho

SPRING TOMATO SOUP
SERVES FOUR

This is a lovely, fresh-tasting soup – it even travels well if you want to take it in a flask on a picnic or a hike in the country. The Italian tomato purée, *passata*, adds a rich smoothness.

INGREDIENTS

1 jar of *passata*, about ¹/₂ litre (20 fl oz)
2 or 3 ripe tomatoes
Bunch spring onions
1–2 tablespoons oil – sunflower or safflower
Pinch sugar
Alpine Salt and pepper
Pinch mint – fresh or dried

METHOD

Trim the spring onions, cut the white bits off, chop finely, put into a large saucepan and fry gently in the oil until pale gold. Cut the green bits into 1-inch (2.5 cm) pieces and put to one side. Chop up the tomatoes, put them in with the onion white bits, add the *passata*, season generously with salt and pepper, add a pinch of sugar, bring it to the boil and simmer for 10 minutes. Add the chopped green bits from the spring onions and the mint, pour into a liquidiser or food processor and whizz for a few seconds, then serve. It is rich red in colour with green flecks, and tastes quite delicious!

POTAGE BONNE FEMME
SERVES·FOUR

This is a simple and delicious soup. I prefer it made with home-made chicken stock, though the late, great Jane Grigson used to say she liked it made with water as she felt stock got in the way of the vegetables.

INGREDIENTS

¹/₂ lb (225 g) each leeks, potatoes, carrots and onions
2 pt (1.2 litres) chicken stock (home-made or stock cube) or water
1 oz (25 g) butter
1 tablespoon fresh chopped parsley
Alpine Salt and pepper

METHOD

Trim the leeks and wash thoroughly. Clean and peel the rest of the vegetables and cut them all into walnut-sized chunks. Melt the butter in a nice big saucepan until it is hot but not brown. Add the vegetables and turn in the butter over a fairly high heat until sizzling and golden. Add the salt and pepper – this gives a much more intense flavour than adding seasonings after the liquid – then put in the stock or water. Simmer gently for 15–20 minutes. Older recipes tell you to simmer for an hour and a half. Do not do it – it destroys all the vitamins! When the vegetables are soft, either mash gently with a fork or process quickly in a food processor or liquidiser until smooth. If you need to, reheat it gently, and serve this lovely creamy soup in bowls with fresh, green parsley sprinkled on top. Lots of hot French bread or toasted granary bread is perfect with this. You may only need some cheese or fruit to follow.

PUMPKIN SOUP

SERVES FOUR

This is a warm and delicious soup that makes the most of all those wonderful pumpkin-related vegetables you can buy these days. You can use just one variety, or mix them a bit.

INGREDIENTS

1 tablespoon oil
1 clove or a teaspoon purée of garlic
1$\frac{1}{2}$ lb (700 g) pumpkin or butternut squash or a mixture of these, with carrots
$\frac{1}{2}$ lb (225 g) each onions and ripe tomatoes
1 tablespoon tomato purée
Good pinch Alpine Salt and pepper
1$\frac{1}{2}$ pt (900 ml) water
Handful croutons and fresh chopped parsley

METHOD

Peel and chop the onions, pumpkin and garlic – and the carrots and squash if you are using them – and chop the tomatoes. Heat the oil in a large saucepan and gently fry the onion until it is just translucent. Add the chopped garlic, let it just soften and then add the pumpkin, carrots and squash together with the tomatoes and tomato purée. Season with salt and pepper, add the water and simmer for 20 minutes. When everything is soft, put it in a blender or food processor and whizz until smooth. Put it back into the saucepan, check the seasoning and serve scattered with croutons and parsley. With fresh granary bread and butter it makes a substantial lunch by itself.

BROCCOLI AND CHEDDAR CHEESE SOUP

SERVES FOUR

This soup looks as good as it tastes, a wonderful deep green with swirls of gold.

INGREDIENTS

1 lb (450 g) fresh broccoli
6 oz (175 g) good mature Cheddar, grated
6 oz (175 g) potatoes
1 medium onion, peeled
1$\frac{1}{2}$ pints (750 ml) chicken stock (a stock cube will do) or water
1 tablespoon sunflower oil
Good pinch Alpine Salt and pepper
$\frac{1}{2}$ teaspoon white sugar

METHOD

Chop the onion, potatoes and broccoli, and put half the florets to one side. Heat the chicken stock or water to boiling point. Pour the oil into a large saucepan, fry the onion very gently until translucent and add the potatoes. Give it a stir, add the boiling chicken stock or water and sugar, and cook the potatoes and onions for about 10 minutes. Add half the broccoli, season and cook until tender – about 5 minutes. Pour it into a blender or food processor with the remaining raw florets, and whizz for a few seconds. When the soup is smooth it will still have a lovely texture from the florets. Now pour the soup back into the saucepan, and stir in the grated Cheddar until that lovely deep green is streaked with gold! Serve with granary or crusty French bread.

TOMATO AND ORANGE SOUP

SERVES FOUR

This is a wonderfully warming summer soup that can be made incredibly quickly. I have given you a couple of recipes; if you like the first, I am sure you will love the second which uses all the lovely squeezed flesh from the oranges as well as the juice. Jars or tetrapacks of *passata* are available in most supermarkets now. It is a smooth purée of Italian tomatoes. Pine nuts are those funny little things that look like half a peanut and taste delicious.

INGREDIENTS

2 tablespoons olive oil
Small onion or bunch spring onions
¹/₂ litre (20 fl oz) *passata*
Alpine Salt and pepper
6–8 fl oz (150–220 ml) freshly squeezed orange juice

METHOD

Put the olive oil into a large saucepan and heat gently. Peel and chop the onion or, if you are using spring onions, trim and chop them finely, keeping some of the green which you can use to garnish the soup. Cook gently until the onion has softened, but do not let it brown. Add the *passata* and half-fill the now empty jar or tetrapack with water – a) because you need the water, and b) it is a good way of getting the last of the *passata* out of the container! Put the water into the saucepan, season generously, stir, bring to the boil and simmer gently for about 15 minutes. You can then purée it, though if the onion was chopped finely enough I do not think it matters. At this point but not before, add the orange juice. It adds a slight sweetness and a sharpness. Do not be tempted to add more than 8 fl oz (220 ml) – it will unbalance the flavours. Let it simmer for just 2–3 minutes. Serve in bowls with a sprinkling of the green bits of the spring onion on top or a little fresh chopped parsley. This is particularly good with wholemeal bread and butter.

WITH PINE NUTS

INGREDIENTS

Juice from 4 fresh oranges, or supermarket equivalent – about a cupful
1 onion
2 tablespoons cooking oil
¹/₂ litre (20 fl oz) *passata*
2 oz (50 g) pine nuts
Alpine Salt and pepper

METHOD

Peel and finely chop the onion, and fry gently in oil in a saucepan until it is translucent. Add the *passata* and the juice and chopped flesh (but not the pips or pith) of the oranges. Season generously. Bring to the boil, turn the heat down and simmer for 20 minutes. In a frying pan heat a little oil and gently fry the pine nuts until they start to go brown. As soon as this happens, stop and remove from the heat. (Pine nuts burn so fast they can be black before you know it.) Check for seasoning. You may need a tiny pinch of sugar at this point. Pour the soup into a bowl and sprinkle with the pine nuts. They add a lovely crunch to a golden, summery soup.

FROM TOP TO BOTTOM: *Pumpkin Soup, Broccoli and Cheddar Cheese Soup, and Tomato and Orange Soup with Pine Nuts*

FRENCH ONION SOUP
SERVES FOUR

This is one of my all-time favourite recipes. It used to be served in Les Halles, that wonderful market in central Paris now banished to the suburbs. The French market porters were said to have drunk this soup early in the morning as it was wonderfully restorative. I use Spanish onions for this soup as they are easier and quicker to handle, but the smaller, more pungent ones (which apparently restored the market porters!) are the traditional onions for this.

INGREDIENTS

1½ lb (700 g) onions, peeled and thinly sliced
1 clove garlic
2 tablespoons oil
1 teaspoon granulated sugar
3 oz (75 g) butter
1½–2 pt (900–1200 ml) good beef stock
Alpine Salt and freshly ground black pepper
4 oz (110 g) grated Gruyère cheese
Thinly sliced French bread

METHOD

Heat the oil in a large, solid saucepan and then melt the butter in the oil. Add the onions and crushed garlic. The trick with this is to cook the onions really slowly. Add the sugar 10 minutes in, and at the end of 30 minutes, the onions should be pale golden brown. The sugar acts to caramelise them and give a rich colour. If the onions are not going brown after about 20 minutes, turn up the heat slightly until they do, but do not let them burn! Pour in the stock with a pinch of salt and black pepper. Bring the soup to the boil and let it simmer for 10 minutes. Heat the oven and put the French bread slices into it until they are dry and crisp. Then pour the soup into bowls. Do not, by the way, use your best china for this soup – you need bowls that will go happily into the oven. Float 2 slices of bread in each bowl and sprinkle the grated Gruyère on top – about 1 oz (25 g) per bowl. Put the bowls into a very hot oven, or under a grill if you prefer, until the cheese is bubbly and melted and the bread is soggy on the bottom but crisp on the top so when you eat it, it is wonderfully nourishing, delicious – and restorative!

BORSCHT
SERVES FOUR

Borscht is *the* Middle European soup, but I have to say it comes in more variations than any other soup I can think of. There are probably no two recipes that agree on what the ingredients should be, except, of course, for the essential one – beetroot. It can be eaten hot, when it is warming and comforting, or in a slightly refined version as a chilled soup.

INGREDIENTS

1½ lb (700 g) beetroot, ready-cooked
1 large onion
1½ pt (900 ml) beef stock or water
1 small green cabbage
2 tablespoons oil, or beef dripping if the soup is to be served hot
Pinch sugar
Alpine Salt and freshly ground black pepper
Sour cream
Chopped chives

METHOD

Peel the cooked beetroot and the onion, and grate them finely. You can do this either in a machine or by hand. Fry the onion and beetroot in either the oil or the dripping. Do not use dripping if you are going to eat this cold; the fat solidifies and is not to be recommended! When the vegetables have softened, add the stock or water. Season generously, bring to the boil and simmer for about 35–40 minutes until everything is so soft it is almost a purée. You can, at this point, add the very finely shredded green cabbage, which gives a lovely variety of texture. Some recipes omit the cabbage altogether, though I think it makes this soup really special. Add the pinch of sugar and cook for another 10 minutes. To serve it hot, pour into individual bowls with a big dollop of sour cream and chopped chives in the middle. To serve it cold, let cool, pour into a food processor and give it a quick whizz. Put it into a bowl and chill in the fridge. Place a couple of ice-cubes into each serving bowl, pour in the chilled borscht, then add the dollop of sour cream and chives. Either way, it is delicious and a very pretty dark red colour.

Borscht

TOP: *Insalata Tricolore*   BOTTOM: *Rainbow Stuffed Eggs* (left) *and Florentine Fennel Spoons*

INSALATA TRICOLORE
SERVES FOUR

The Italian flag is green, red and white. So is this simple, clear-tasting salad of creamy avocado, smooth mozzarella and the sweet bite of tomato. The very large beef tomatoes are best for this salad.

INGREDIENTS

2 large ripe avocados
2 beef tomatoes
½ lb (250 g) mozzarella cheese
A little shredded lettuce
For the dressing
4 tablespoons olive oil
2 tablespoons lemon juice
Pinch sugar
Pinch Alpine Salt

METHOD

Peel the avocados, halve them and take out the stones. Put each avocado half face down on a plate and slice it vertically and thinly. Push down on it slightly and it will turn into a fan. Slice the tomatoes and the mozzarella equally thinly and fan out the slices by each avocado half. And there you have the green, red and white of the Italian flag. Decorate with a little shredded lettuce. Mix the dressing ingredients together, pour over the salad and put in the fridge for about half an hour for the flavours to develop. Avoid pouring the dressing over the lettuce – it will go soggy! Serve with that lovely crusty Italian bread, *ciabatta*.

FLORENTINE FENNEL SPOONS
SERVES FOUR

Fennel has a lovely crisp texture like celery, but has a tiny aniseedy flavour. It makes a wonderful starter because, when opened carefully, it turns into giant vegetable spoons which you can fill with all kinds of goodies.

INGREDIENTS

1 unblemished head of fennel
8–10 oz (225–275 g) cottage cheese or Italian ricotta
Bunch spring onions
1 tablespoon fresh basil, chopped
Juice of half a lemon
1 tablespoon olive oil
Alpine Salt and black pepper

METHOD

Trim the sharp end of the fennel, leaving as much of the stick as possible. At the other end, remove the base so you can peel off each 'leaf' which will look like a large vegetable spoon, with a little handle. They do get smaller, but you should be able to get 4 big spoons off before you reach the heart. Finely chop the heart and 2 spring onions, and mix them in with the cheese, the olive oil, chopped basil and lemon juice. Season generously with salt and black pepper. Then pile it back into the fennel spoons until it is mounded up high. This is low fat, delicious and crunchy – the lemon juice spikes it, the cheese makes it creamy, it looks very pretty and it tastes marvellous with just that slight hint of aniseed to freshen the whole thing.

RAINBOW STUFFED EGGS
SERVES FOUR

This is a nice, multi-coloured starter. It is a version of egg mayonnaise, but much prettier! I use free-range eggs – it makes a big difference to the flavour, and a huge difference to the chicken. There are three coloured flavourings for this dish – red, green and gold.

INGREDIENTS

6 large eggs

6 tablespoons mayonnaise, preferably home-made, otherwise a good bought one

For the red eggs	*For the gold eggs*
1 teaspoon tomato purée	1 tablespoon mango chutney
$^1/_2$ teaspoon dried basil	$^1/_2$ teaspoon curry powder
Alpine Salt and pepper	Alpine Salt and pepper

For the green eggs

4 anchovy fillets

1 tablespoon finely chopped parsley

METHOD

Put the eggs into cold water, bring them to the boil and simmer for 10 minutes. When they are cooked, run them under cold water and crack the shells immediately. This keeps the whites white and the yolks yellow. Cut them in half lengthways and remove the yolks.

Place all the whites in neat rows. Put all the yolks together and mash them with the mayonnaise. Divide the yolk mixture into three and put each third into a separate bowl. Into one, mix in the tomato and basil flavouring, with plenty of salt and pepper. Into the next, mix in the parsley and anchovies. And into the third, mix in the mango chutney, curry powder and seasoning. Then all you do is fill the middle of the whites with the colourings, so you have 4 whites with red middles, 4 with green and 4 with gold. Put a little bed of shredded lettuce on to 4 plates and lay 3 egg halves on each plate, so each person has one in each colour. You could put a little cherry tomato in the centre of the 3 eggs to make it even prettier.

What could be nicer or more simple?

SPINACH AND FETA PARCELS
SERVES FOUR

These are little parcels of that lovely, thin, crispy filo pastry, filled with spinach and feta cheese and a little spice. It is simple, effective and makes a very good first course.

INGREDIENTS

$^1/_2$ lb (225 g) feta cheese
$1^1/_2$ lb (700 g) fresh or $^1/_2$ lb (225 g) frozen leaf spinach (which is the Crafty way to cook this)
16 sheets (or 1 packet) filo pastry
1 onion
Pinch ground nutmeg
2 oz (50 g) butter
1 tablespoon oil
Pinch Alpine Salt

METHOD

If the spinach is fresh, wash it, then wilt it in boiling water for a couple of minutes and drain it. If frozen, defrost gently, and drain well. Mix the spinach with half the butter. Peel and finely chop the onion and fry in the oil until softened. Mix it in with the spinach and butter. Add the pinch of nutmeg. Put the remaining butter into a saucepan and melt it gently. Spread one sheet of filo out flat and brush with melted butter. Put another piece of filo on top, but at right angles to the first, so you now have an eight-pointed star of pastry. Put one-eighth of the spinach mixture into the middle of the filo star and put a couple of half-inch (1 cm) cubes of feta on top, with a pinch of salt. Bring the sides of the star together so they meet in the middle and give them a gentle twist to make a little parcel. Brush the outside lightly with a little melted butter. Repeat until you have 8 small parcels. Put them on a lightly greased and floured baking sheet in a hot oven, gas mark 7 / 425°F / 210°C / 190°C fan-assisted oven, or the top of an Aga roasting oven for approximately 20 minutes. Watch carefully to make sure that the tips of the filo parcels do not burn. If they start to, just put a little greaseproof paper over the tips for the rest of the cooking time. Take them out and you have this marvellous combination of crispy pastry, melting cheese and beautifully hot spinach and onion. They can be eaten hot, which is my favourite, or cold – but do not put them in the fridge, they will just go soggy!

Spinach and Feta Parcels

GUACAMOLE
<u>SERVES FOUR</u>

This can either be a first course or something to eat with, say, Chilli con Carne or Mexican Rice. It does, in fact, come from Mexico, which was a huge market garden when Columbus got there. Avocados, red and green peppers and tomatoes all grew and were developed in the Yucatan Peninsula, and came to us from there.

INGREDIENTS

1 large ripe avocado
1 red pepper
1 green pepper
Bunch spring onions
1 large tomato or 2–3 ordinary ones, skinned and de-seeded
Juice of a lime
2 tablespoons oil
Alpine Salt
Pinch ground chilli pepper

METHOD

Trim the spring onions and de-seed the peppers. Chop them really finely, either with a sharp knife or a very quick whizz in a food processor. Cut the avocado in half lengthways and unscrew it, as it were, to halve it and remove the stone. Scoop out the flesh into a glass or china bowl and mash with a fork. Add the lime juice and season generously with salt and the chilli pepper, if you are brave enough to use it. Mix in the chopped vegetables, which should be almost liquid, and the result is a pale green purée. Add a little oil so it is the consistency of thick double cream. For a starter, line individual dishes with lettuce leaf cups, pile the guacamole into them and serve with tortilla chips. To eat with a main course, spoon the guacamole into a big bowl in the centre of the table so people can dip in and use it as a sauce when eating something spicy.

BUTTERED HERBED MUSHROOMS

SERVES FOUR TO SIX

I first came across this as a teenager visiting Lyon, the gastronomic capital of France. The dinner I remember most vividly began with a great pile of these buttered, herbed mushrooms. For this recipe I use chestnut mushrooms – dark brown, organically grown, with a really substantial flavour.

INGREDIENTS

1$^1/_2$ lb (700 g) chestnut mushrooms
3 oz (75 g) butter
2 tablespoons each chopped fresh parsley and chopped fresh chives
$^1/_2$ clove garlic, finely chopped
Alpine Salt and freshly ground black pepper

METHOD

Trim the mushrooms with a sharp knife, but do not peel them. Put them in a colander and sterilise by pouring a kettleful of boiling water over them. If the mushrooms are big, cut them in halves or quarters. Heat the butter in a large pan, put in the chopped garlic and soften it gently for a couple of minutes. Add the mushrooms, put the lid on and cook for not more than 1$^1/_2$ minutes on maximum heat. The mushrooms steam but do not become gloppy. They should be crisp and hot and garlicky. Season at this point and sprinkle on the parsley and chopped chives. Pile the mushrooms on each person's plate in a little mountain not less than 2 inches (5 cm) high. That fits my memory perfectly!

STILTON AND MANGO TOAST

SERVES FOUR

This is the most exotic cheese on toast you have ever tasted and designed for when you really do not feel like cooking, but want to eat something nice. It is one of my favourite supper dishes, but you could serve smaller portions at the end of a grand dinner party as a savoury, or even at the beginning as a starter! I think it is best made with wholemeal bread, but white will do. Either way, it is improved if the bread has been sliced by you, not by a machine.

INGREDIENTS

4 large slices bread
4 large tablespoons good mango chutney
$^1/_2$ lb (225 g) blue Stilton
1 oz (25 g) butter

METHOD

Toast the bread, and butter it as if it were breakfast. Then spread the buttered side of each piece with the mango chutney, so it goes right to the very edge – this is most important. If you toasted the bread in a toaster, pre-heat the grill now to its highest setting. Crumble the Stilton and put it on top of the chutney, again making sure it goes right to the edges. Press the cheese down slightly so it does not fall off. Put it under the hot grill, about 2 inches (5 cm) away from the heat, for 4–5 minutes until the Stilton is golden and bubbling. When you eat it, you get a wonderful almost sweet and sour flavour, with the toast giving it some substance. If really hungry, you may feel that 2 pieces per person is more appropriate!

EGGS

SPANISH OMELETTE
SERVES FOUR

This is a great user up of left-over bits. It is very quick, very filling, and as delicious as the ingredients you choose to put in it.

INGREDIENTS

6 eggs
1½ lb (700 g) potatoes
1½ lb (700 g) onions
½ lb (225 g) frozen exotic mixed vegetables
Plus anything odd in the fridge – cooked meat, fish, sausage, etc.
2 tablespoons oil
1 teaspoon fresh or dried herbs

METHOD

Scrub, slice, then boil the potatoes until just tender – about 15 minutes. Chop the cooked meat, fish or sausage you are adding into small pieces. Peel and slice the onions. Heat the oil in a big frying pan and gently fry the onions until just beginning to turn golden. Add the sliced potatoes, then the frozen vegetables, stir and cook for a minute while you beat the eggs until just frothy, and then add them to the pan. Gently mix it all together and cook over a medium to high heat for 2–3 minutes. Now add the goodies from the fridge and the teaspoon of fresh or dried herbs. The egg should now be firm and everything else hot through. Put the pan under the grill for 1–2 minutes until the top of the omelette is brown and bubbly. For supper or lunch, just serve a green salad with this, and lots of crusty French bread and butter.

EGG MOUSSE
SERVES FOUR

This can be a starter or, with salad and bread and butter, a light lunch dish. It is very delicate, easy, and looks as pretty as it tastes delicious!

INGREDIENTS

3 hard-boiled eggs
2 spring onions or 1 tablespoon chopped fresh chives
1 teaspoon lemon juice
1 standard tin concentrated consommé
6 tablespoons mayonnaise
Pinch Alpine Salt and freshly ground black pepper

METHOD

Melt the consommé gently in a saucepan – do not bring to the boil – remove from the heat and add lemon juice. As soon as it has cooled, chill it in the fridge. Trim the spring onions, shell the eggs, cut them in half and put the onions (or chives) and eggs into a liquidiser or food processor. Process for a few seconds, scrape down the sides, add the consommé mixture, mayonnaise and seasoning, and process for a few more seconds until thoroughly blended. It will be a pale golden colour with lovely green flecks from the spring onions or chives. Do not over-process – this is much nicer with a slight texture. Pour it all into a soufflé dish and allow to set in the fridge for at least 2 hours, preferably 4, to make sure the whole lot goes firm. It can even be left overnight in the fridge, covered with cling film. This is nicest spooned out from the dish, not sliced, and eaten with granary or wholemeal toast.

TOP: *Spanish Omelette*   BOTTOM: *Classic seasoning from the Alps*

FRENCH OMELETTE WITH MELTED CHEESE AND CROUTONS

SERVES ONE

This is simple, economic and quite delicious. It is the classic folded French omelette, with a slightly unusual and very yummy filling. The great trick when making a French omelette is the size of the pan. French omelettes are best made thicker than you expect. So for a 3-egg omelette you need a 5-inch (13 cm) pan; for 6 eggs, a 10-inch (25.5 cm) pan; and for 12 eggs, a 12-inch (30 cm) pan. If you are cooking more eggs you are on your own! The best omelette I ever had was cooked on a French train and served 14 people for breakfast. I have spent my life trying to copy it! The quantities are per person – you can make 2 or 3 of these very quickly.

INGREDIENTS

3 large eggs
1 oz (25 g) grated cheese – Gruyère is best, Cheddar is fine, Lancashire is good as it does not go stringy when it melts
A walnut-sized knob of butter
Alpine Salt and black pepper
For the croutons, per person
1/2 slice white bread
1 tablespoon oil

METHOD

Start by making the croutons. Cut the bread into small squares of about half to a quarter of an inch (1 cm – 5 mm). Fry in the oil gently and take them out as soon as they turn golden. Wipe the pan out and put in the butter. In a bowl lightly beat the 3 eggs. Heat the butter until it foams and hisses, pour in the 3 beaten eggs and, with the back of a fork, scramble them in the hot butter for about a minute until all the egg is cooked. When it looks sort of soft-scrambled, put on the cheese, sprinkle over the croutons, and season it. While the middle is still a little moist, fold it with a palette knife or a fork and tip it on to a warm plate. The omelette will go on cooking for another 35 seconds to a minute so take it out of the pan just before it is cooked. It is a wonderful omelette, slightly soft in the middle, crunchy and cheesy, and I eat it with a green salad with a good French dressing.

CAROLINE'S CHEESE PUDDING

SERVES FOUR

This is a cheese soufflé at cottage garden level. It is easy to do and there are no problems about whether it will rise or not. It is named after a friend of mine who first gave me the recipe nearly 20 years ago as a delicious lunch or supper dish. It is light, but warm.

To make it you need bread from a real loaf, not one of the sliced things. It does not have to be brown, white is absolutely fine for this; and if it is a bit stale, that does not matter either!

INGREDIENTS

2 thick slices of bread
4 oz (110 g) good cheese – Cheddar or Gruyère are best
2 large eggs
$^1/_2$ pt (300 ml) milk
1 dessertspoon French mustard
Alpine Salt and freshly ground black pepper
Fresh chopped chives or parsley – optional

METHOD

You first need to turn the bread into breadcrumbs. I prefer using a food processor for something soft like breadcrumbs, rather than a grater, as the latter tends to be a bit tough on fingers! Grate the cheese – graters are fine with hard cheese – and mix the cheese and breadcrumbs together. Soak them in the milk and stir in the mustard. Season with salt and pepper. Separate the eggs and beat the yolks into the cheese, bread, milk and mustard mixture. Whip the whites together in a clean bowl until they are really stiff. Fold the whites into the cheesy mixture and, at this point, you could gently fold in a handful of chopped chives or parsley if you like green in your soufflé. Put the mixture into a buttered soufflé dish or an old-fashioned pie dish. Put it into a medium oven, gas mark 5 / 375°F / 190°C / 170°C fan-assisted or the middle of an Aga roasting oven for about 45 minutes. It will rise not as spectacularly as a real soufflé, but it will rise quite a lot. It will look lovely and golden at the top and the inside will be soft, cheesy and scrumptious. I do not think it needs anything with it. It is a course on its own, either as a light main dish with salad and fruit to follow, or as a starter for six people.

SMOKED SALMON AND SCRAMBLED EGGS

SERVES FOUR

This is an unusual combination of great luxury and great cheapness. It was developed in New York as a breakfast dish, but I like it for lunch or as a light supper. You can also serve it as a splendid first course. It is very easy to make and the great Crafty secret is that you do not need sheets of expensive smoked salmon. What you need is smoked salmon scraps, which many fishmongers or specialist delicatessens sell at literally a fraction of the price of the big slices. You can also buy them pre-packed in most big supermarkets.

INGREDIENTS

½ lb (225 g) smoked salmon bits
12 large eggs, preferably free-range
3 oz (75 g) butter
1 tablespoon fresh or freeze-dried chopped chives
Alpine Salt and freshly ground black pepper

METHOD

Trim the smoked salmon scraps of any bony or finny bits and any skin. Cut them into matchstick-sized pieces. Melt the butter in a big non-stick pan until it hisses and then stops hissing. At the instant it stops – be quick as it is about to go brown which you do not want – put in half the smoked salmon strips. In a separate bowl, beat the eggs lightly. When the cooking smoked salmon is just beginning to perfume the air, pour in the eggs and stir with a wooden spoon until the mixture begins to turn crumbly but is still slightly moist. Add the chives and almost all the rest of the smoked salmon – keep a teaspoonful or two back for decoration. Stir the egg mixture quickly and, while it is still moist and slightly soft, heap it on to slices of fresh, granary toast or pile it into small, warmed bowls and serve the toast separately. Season it with just a little salt and freshly ground black pepper, and sprinkle the last bits of smoked salmon on the top. It is the most luxurious and delicious dish, and looks very pretty too.

Smoked Salmon and Scrambled Eggs

ANGLESEY EGGS

SERVES FOUR

This is a very simple Welsh dish that makes the most of leeks when they are at their peak in late March, early April.

INGREDIENTS

1 pt (600 ml) milk, or $^1/_2$ pt (300 ml) milk and $^1/_2$ pt (300 ml) single cream
$1^1/_2$ lb (700 g) leeks
8 free-range eggs
1 heaped tablespoon cornflour
$^1/_2$ teaspoon Alpine Salt
1 oz (25 g) butter
Pinch nutmeg
1–2 oz (25–50 g) grated Caerphilly or Cheddar cheese

METHOD

Clean the leeks, trim top and bottom, but do not remove the green leaves. Cut into 1-inch (2.5 cm) lengths. Put the milk or milk and cream into a non-stick saucepan, add the leeks and bring to the boil. If you like your leeks soft rather than slightly crisp, let them boil for a minute or two. Take the leeks out of the saucepan (leaving the milk in the pan), strain off any excess liquid and put into a baking dish. Place the eggs into boiling water and cook for exactly 5 minutes. (If you are worried about the eggs cracking as they meet the boiling water, you could alternatively put them into cold water, bring to the boil, turn off the heat and let them stand for 6 minutes.) Take the eggs out, cool, and shell carefully. This is much easier than poaching – the French call them *oeufs mollets*. The eggs should be soft in the middle but the whites firm. Halve the shelled eggs and put them on top of the leeks. With the milk (or milk and cream) which you have left in the saucepan, make a white sauce by whisking in the cornflour, salt and butter, and bring gently to the boil while you whisk – this is an easy way to make white sauce. Pour over the eggs and leeks, sprinkle with the nutmeg and cheese, and put under the grill just until it is hot and bubbling. Don't leave it too long or the eggs will be overcooked. Serve at once with lots of granary bread and butter.

 ISH

STIR-FRIED PRAWNS WITH SNOWPEAS

SERVES FOUR

There is a good range of flat, eat-all peas in most supermarkets and greengrocers. There are two kinds – the really flat mangetout and the American snowpeas or sugar-snaps, which are slightly sweeter and have a fatter pod.

INGREDIENTS

½ lb (225g) snowpeas
1 clove garlic
1 small piece fresh ginger
Bunch spring onions
12 oz (350 g) small raw prawns (you can use cooked if necessary)
1 tablespoon soy sauce
1 tablespoon sugar
1 tablespoon lemon juice
½ tablespoon cornflour
2 tablespoons oil

METHOD

Peel and chop the ginger and the garlic. Wash and trim the spring onions and cut into 1-inch (2.5 cm) lengths. Top and tail the snowpeas. Heat the oil in a large saucepan or wok, and fry the garlic and ginger quickly; do not let them brown. If using raw prawns, fry them until pink. If using cooked prawns, do not add them yet. Add the spring onions and snowpeas and turn (stir-fry) the whole lot for about 2 minutes. Mix in a cup the soy sauce, the lemon juice, the sugar and the cornflour, and add enough water until it is the thickness of single cream. Pour it into the pan, then stir and toss it until suddenly it is glossy and golden. If you are using cooked prawns, add them now. Turn them a couple of times until well mixed in. Serve this lovely, golden, green and glossy dish with plenty of boiled rice.

TOP: *Stir-fried Prawns with Snowpeas*   BOTTOM: *Barbecued Fish*

Cod Portuguese

COD PORTUGUESE
SERVES FOUR

Gaze out to sea in Portugal and there is nothing between you and America. It is an Atlantic country, with fishing grounds much like ours. Would that we had a similar climate! The Portuguese cook fish marvellously, using a particular mixture of tomatoes and onions, which the French have decided – rightly, it must be said – is the Portuguese culinary signature.

INGREDIENTS

1½ lb (700 g) filleted cod or cod cutlets
1 lb (450 g) Spanish onions
1 lb (450 g) ripe French or Italian plum tomatoes, fresh if you can get them, otherwise tinned (and chopped)
4 tablespoons olive oil
Large handful chopped parsley
Alpine Salt and freshly ground black pepper

METHOD

Trim the pieces of cod and skin them if you can. Heat the olive oil in a large pan in which you can lay all the pieces of cod, and fry them very gently for 2 minutes each side, just to seal the fish. Peel and slice the onions finely and crumble them all over the cod. If you are using fresh tomatoes, skin them and chop with a knife on a board or in a bowl so you get as much juice as possible. Add the tomatoes to the pan, season generously, cover with a lid and cook gently for 15–20 minutes, depending on the thickness of the cod. Do not let the fish overcook. The tomatoes should turn into a kind of mush, and the onions go translucent. This is not meant to be a liquid sauce, but one where you can still see and taste the characteristics of the vegetables. Take the fish out and put on to warmed plates. Add the handful of chopped parsley to the sauce mixture and stir it around until it is thoroughly mixed so the sauce has a lovely golden, red and green colouring. Pour that over the cod in each individual portion. Do not be tempted to add anything else – the combination of the simple flavours is what works best in this dish. If, by the way, it has occurred to you that Spanish onions, and French or Italian tomatoes with Portuguese cod makes this something of a Euro-dish, you could always go one better and serve it with plain boiled or steamed Irish potatoes!

BARBECUED FISH
SERVES FOUR

This marinade recipe is for any fish, but is particularly good with oily fish like herrings and mackerel – cheap – or trout or small pieces of salmon – not quite so cheap! What you also need, apart from a properly lit barbecue, is a long-handled, fish-shaped grid which holds the fish so you can turn it easily.

INGREDIENTS

2 lb (1 kg) fish (allowing $1/2$ lb or 225 g per person)
4 tablespoons olive oil
Juice of a lemon
1 bay leaf
2 peppercorns
1 fresh or dried chilli
1 tablespoon soy sauce

METHOD

Put all the marinade ingredients into a bowl big enough to hold the fish, mix together, then bury the fish in it, turning 2 or 3 times. If you can leave it for up to 24 hours in the fridge, it comes out tasting more than a bit scrumptious, but even just 2 hours will improve it greatly. The marinade also adds a coating which helps stop the fish sticking on the barbecue. It is very important to get the barbecue very hot, but not flaming – the flames should have died down before you put on any food. If you are using the grid – and it really is well worthwhile getting one – oil it carefully and get it very hot before you put the fish in it, so when you do, the fish seals where it touches the wire. Grill for about 10 minutes, turning once or twice. The idea is for the skin to be crisp, charred and golden, and the flesh still succulent inside. You can test this by prodding just behind the head – or, if you are squeamish, where the head used to be – with a skewer. The flesh should just flake. Remember, fish will go on cooking after it is taken off the barbecue. Put the fish on a plate, give it a last brushing with the marinade, and serve with crusty French bread, and a salad to follow. Do not serve the salad on the same plate, you will never separate the fish bones from the frisée!

Barbecue table showing, from left to right, Salade Niçoise, Salad with Walnuts and Walnut Oil, Rice Salad, and Focaccio. Also shown are Lamb Saté and Sasatis (prepared for the barbecue) and fresh trout.

SALMON
SERVES FOUR

The grandest way to serve salmon is to cook a whole fish – you can buy anything from a 2–3 lb (1–1.35 kg) salmon upwards relatively cheaply – and it is perfect for a dinner party or family lunch. The traditional way to cook a whole fish is in a fish kettle but most people do not have one. I, and almost everyone else I know, wrap it in foil and it cooks very satisfactorily in the oven. An alternative is to buy salmon pieces and these can be poached in a large saucepan. But there is a trick to perfect poaching. Wrap the salmon piece in a safe and suitable cling film before you put it into the water or *court bouillon* – it keeps a perfect shape and does not go either watery or dry. Serve with new potatoes, Hollandaise Sauce (see opposite) and strawberry and cucumber salad (Salade Elana – see page 127).

POACHED SALMON

INGREDIENTS

2 lb (1 kg) piece of salmon, or
4 cutlets

For the court bouillon

1/2 lemon

4 peppercorns

1 1/2 pt (900 ml) water

Bay leaf

Pinch Alpine Salt

METHOD

Put all the ingredients for the *court bouillon* into a large saucepan, bring to the boil and simmer for about 10–15 minutes. Allow to cool slightly. Wrap the salmon in cling film, place carefully in the warm liquid, bring to the boil, and simmer gently for just 6 minutes to the pound (450 g). Turn off the heat and leave it for the same length of time again; i.e. simmer a 2 lb (1 kg) salmon for 12 minutes, then leave it turned off for another 12. The salmon will be perfectly cooked. If you want to serve it cold, leave to cool completely in the water before unwrapping it – that way it stays beautifully moist. To serve hot, carefully unwrap it, gently remove the skin, and put it on to warm plates.

BAKED SALMON

INGREDIENTS

2–3 lb (1–1.35 kg) salmon

1 lemon

Alpine Salt and pepper

METHOD

Take a piece of silver foil large enough to wrap the salmon in a very loose parcel. Slice a lemon thinly and lay about half on the bottom of the foil. Put the salmon on top, with a few slices of lemon inside and the rest on top of the salmon. Season with salt and pepper, and wrap loosely, but make sure the edges are securely folded together so no steam can escape. Put into a medium oven, gas mark 4 / 350°F / 180°C / 160°C fan-assisted oven, for 10 minutes per pound (450 g). If serving hot, take it out of the oven and let stand in the foil for a further 10 minutes. If serving cold, leave the salmon in the foil for 2–3 hours until it is cold; that way the fish stays moist. Before serving, unwrap the fish and gently pull off the skin. Put it on the biggest plate you have. You can decorate it with slices of cucumber or a few sprigs of watercress.

HOLLANDAISE SAUCE

This is the very best sauce to serve with hot salmon, and is simple to make if you have a liquidiser or food processor. The traditional way is in a *bain marie* and takes about 15 minutes. The Crafty way is in a non-stick saucepan and takes about three! A word of warning – it is made with raw egg so is not advisable for the elderly, the pregnant, or for very young children.

INGREDIENTS

1 whole egg and 1 yolk
Pinch Alpine Salt
Juice of half a lemon
Small pinch white pepper
$^{1}/_{2}$ lb (225 g) butter

METHOD

Into the liquidiser or food processor put the egg and egg yolk, salt, lemon juice and a little white pepper. Process it briefly. In a non-stick saucepan heat the butter – I prefer it slightly salted but you can use unsalted which is traditional. Heat until it sizzles. The moment it stops sizzling, switch on the liquidiser and pour the melted butter through the little hole in the top in a continuous stream, leaving out the gloppy white bits at the bottom – do not pour in the last few drops. Process in the liquidiser for about 30 seconds. Throw out the little white bits in the saucepan, quickly wipe the saucepan and pour the sauce back in, but do not put it back on the heat. Stir the sauce in the hot saucepan for about 25–30 seconds until it coats the back of the spoon. You will find the heat from the pan finishes the thickening process and you will have perfect Hollandaise. If you need to keep it warm before serving, put it in a bowl over a saucepan of hot water on a low heat. Do not try to reheat in a saucepan over direct heat – if you do you will have very expensive scrambled eggs!

Salmon prepared for the oven

Fresh Salmon Pâté

FRESH SALMON PÂTÉ

SERVES FOUR AS A MAIN DISH, EIGHT TO TEN AS A
STARTER

This is really a little bit more than a pâté; it is almost
potted salmon in the sumptuous 18th-century manner. It
can be eaten as a first course or, the way I like it, as a lunch
or supper dish served with tiny new potatoes and a really
delicious salad. If you cannot get your salmon skinned, the
cooking process makes it easy to lift off.

INGREDIENTS

$1\frac{1}{2}$ lb (700 g) salmon, boned and skinned

$\frac{1}{2}$ lb (225 g) butter

1 teaspoon each of Alpine Salt and ground white
pepper

$\frac{1}{2}$ teaspoon each of ground cloves, ground mace or
nutmeg, and ground bay leaves

A little fresh lemon juice

Chopped parsley or chives for decoration

METHOD

Check that as many bones as possible really have been removed,
then put the salmon into a large saucepan of cold water with a
pinch of salt and a squeeze of lemon juice. Bring to the boil and
poach for approximately 10–15 minutes – one large piece of salmon
will take longer than a couple of smaller pieces. Turn off the heat
and allow the salmon to cool in the water for a further 10 minutes.
If the skin is still on, you will find it lifts away effortlessly at this
point. Put the salmon in a big bowl, and mash with a fork, or use a
food processor. Gently melt the butter in a saucepan and add to it
all the other seasonings – the ground bay leaves, white pepper,
cloves, mace or nutmeg, and the salt. Stir and pour it into the
salmon. If you are using a food processor, give it a quick whizz,
otherwise stir with a fork until it is thoroughly amalgamated. If you
want to slice the salmon, spoon it into a loaf-shaped container lined
with cling film. If you want to serve it as a pâté, put it into a round
soufflé dish. Sprinkle with a little parsley or chives for a lovely
contrasting colour, and chill for at least 4 hours. You can then turn
it out of the loaf-shaped tin and slice it into the most delicious pale
pink pâté as a main course, or scoop it out of the soufflé dish with a
spoon and eat it on hot crunchy toast or crusty French bread as a
starter. And if it sounds rich, believe me, it is!

FISH PIE

SERVES FOUR

This pie is particularly attractive because the smoked fish gives it that little extra texture, flavour and colour. Coley is the cheapest white fish, and makes an extremely good fish pie. You can use cod, of which coley is a relative, or big whiting, or even halibut! For the smoked haddock, buy the naturally-coloured fish, not the dyed yellow kind.

INGREDIENTS

1 lb (450 g) white fish, skinned and boned
1 lb (450 g) smoked haddock, skinned and boned
2 small onions or ½ Spanish onion, finely chopped
½ lb (225 g) button mushrooms
½ pt (300 ml) full-cream milk or even ½ pt (300 ml) single cream!
1½ lb (700 g) mashing potatoes
2½ oz (60 g) butter
1½ oz (40 g) plain flour
Good pinch grated nutmeg
Alpine Salt and pepper

METHOD

Peel and cut the potatoes into chunks and boil in plenty of salted water until soft enough to mash. Put all the boned and skinned fish into the milk or cream, and poach gently for a couple of minutes until it stiffens. Do not cook it fully just yet. Scald the mushrooms in boiling water to clean them, and cut into quarters. Take the fish out of the milk or cream and flake it into chunks. Into the milk/cream, whisk the flour and just over half of the butter. Add the pinch of nutmeg, seasoning – watch the amount of salt as there may be some in the smoked fish – and whisk over the heat until it becomes a thick sauce. Add the button mushrooms and the flaked fish to the sauce and pour into a pie dish. Put a layer of chopped onion on top. Drain and mash the cooked potatoes with the remaining butter, season and then, spoonful by spoonful, cover the top of the onion and fish, smoothing gently with a fork. Put the dish into a medium oven, gas mark 4 / 350°F / 180°C / 160°C fan-assisted oven, or the middle of an Aga roasting oven for about 25–30 minutes until the top is just starting to go crispy brown and the sauce is bubbling underneath. The layers of flavour in this are just delicious. You do not want anything else at all with the pie, but you might like to serve a green vegetable or salad afterwards.

TROUT ALMONDINE

SERVES FOUR

Trout in my youth used to be something of a luxury, but because of trout farms it has become cheap and very good value. No longer do trout have a muddy taste and appearance, rather they are a delicate pink like a pale salmon. Almonds are the traditional accompaniment to trout. This recipe is trout double almondine!

INGREDIENTS

4 prepared trout, about 6–8 oz (175–225 g) each
4 tablespoons ground almonds
2 tablespoons oil (not olive oil)
2 tablespoons butter
Juice of a lemon
2 oz (50 g) slivered almonds
Alpine Salt and pepper

METHOD

Put the ground almonds with salt and pepper into a plastic or paper bag of some substance. Trim the trout, put them into the bag and shake it so the trout are coated with the almonds. Heat the oil in a frying pan large enough to hold all the trout, then add the butter and let it melt until it stops sizzling. Put the almonded trout into the frying pan and cook over a medium heat for 3–4 minutes each side.

Fry them until they are golden and the flesh is flaking. Take the trout out and put on to a warm plate. Into the pan put the slivered almonds and turn the heat up quickly so they just start to go pale brown. Pour the butter and the slivered almonds over the trout, so you have two layers of almonds, and squeeze the lemon over the top. If you are a purist, you could squeeze the lemon juice into the pan and swirl it about so it picks up all the lovely sticky bits left behind. This goes marvellously with cucumber pieces tossed in a little butter in a saucepan and Focaccio bread (see opposite and page 166).

TOP: *Trout Almondine served with buttered cucumber*   BOTTOM: *Focaccio*

BAKED STUFFED TOMATOES WITH PRAWNS

SERVES FOUR

I make this dish in double quantities, one lot to have hot for dinner as a main course, the other to have cold the next day as a starter. For years big tomatoes never tasted the same when bought here as they did just 30 miles across the sea in Calais. They still do not quite, but they are definitely travelling much better than they used to!

INGREDIENTS

4 large tomatoes
Bunch spring onions
6 oz (175 g) cooked long-grain rice
1 tablespoon oil
2 tablespoons raisins
1 tablespoon chopped fresh parsley
4 oz (110 g) shelled, cooked prawns
Alpine Herb Salt and freshly ground black pepper

METHOD

Cut a lid off each tomato about half an inch (1 cm) thick. Keep the lid. Over a sieve, scoop out all the pulp and juice from inside the tomatoes, so you are left with the solid bits. Put the tomato shells on one side and upside down so they drain. Wash the onions, chop them (including the green bits), and fry them in the oil in a large frying pan or saucepan for about a minute. Add the cooked rice, the raisins, the parsley and the drained pulp of tomato. Give it a thorough stir round until it is hot. Add half the prawns and mix together. Put the tomato shells in an ovenproof dish, fill them with the rice and prawn mixture and season generously. Put the lids on, drizzle them with a little oil, and cook in an oven on gas mark 4 / 350°F / 180°C / 160°C fan-assisted oven, or the bottom of an Aga roasting oven for 35 minutes. (Half way through the cooking time, remove from the oven and place the rest of the prawns round the tops of the tomatoes in a decorative spiral, to garnish.) If you like a little sauce, you may want to pour a cup of water round them, otherwise, line the baking dish with buttered greaseproof paper so they do not stick. They are delicious hot or cold.

HADDOCK PAPRIKACHE
SERVES FOUR

This is a Middle European fish dish, very easy to make. You can make it with fillets of cod, whiting or coley as well as haddock! Get your fishmonger to fillet the fish and skin it as well – though this is not essential. Most big supermarkets now sell a good variety of fresh pre-packed fish if there is no fishmonger near you.

INGREDIENTS

1½ lb (700 g) fillets of white fish
1 lb (450 g) Spanish onions
1 heaped tablespoon paprika
Alpine Salt and pepper
10 fl oz (300 ml) double cream

METHOD

Make sure there are no obvious bones left in the fish fillets. Peel the onions and slice them thinly. In a baking dish place a layer of onions, a layer of fish, a layer of onions and a layer of fish. Mix the paprika, salt and pepper into the cream, stir it well and pour over the fish. Cover with buttered foil and bake in a medium oven, gas mark 4 / 350°F / 180°C / 160°C fan-assisted oven, or the bottom of an Aga roasting oven. Cook for about 35–40 minutes. The cream, the fish and the onions blend into a most wonderful rose-pink coloured mixture. You can eat it with rice, with noodles or – my favourite – mashed potato!

HERRINGS IN OATMEAL
SERVES FOUR

Herrings used to be the basic fare during Lent in medieval England, and were brought to shore from the North Sea in their thousands. Conservation was not a consideration! This is a lovely toasty way to cook herrings. The oatmeal you need is the real stuff; instant porridge will not do!

INGREDIENTS

4 fat herrings
4 dessertspoons Alpine Salt
4 dessertspoons oatmeal

METHOD

Cover the base of a large, solid frying pan with a thin layer of salt. Heat the pan until the salt just starts to brown. Put the fish in on top of the salt. The salt will draw the herring oils out and will fry the fish in its own oil. Turn the fish after 3 or 4 minutes. After a further 2 minutes add the oatmeal, scattering it over the fish. The oatmeal absorbs the remaining oil and goes crisp like toasted almonds. Serve these wonderful, crispy-skinned herrings with just a squeeze of lemon juice and a little freshly ground black pepper.

DRESSED CRAB

SERVES FOUR AS A STARTER, TWO AS A MAIN DISH

Unlike lobster, which has become ridiculously expensive, you can still buy a large crab for around £2 and turn it into the most delicious summer dish. You can buy fresh, cooked crab in two forms. If it is totally unprepared, weigh it in your hand. If the crab is heavy but sounds sloshy, as if it were full of water, it is. What you want is one that is heavy, i.e. full of meat, but does not slosh. The other way to buy crab is semi-prepared, which many supermarkets and fishmongers now do – the crab has been opened, the grotty bits taken out and the white and the brown meat separated.

INGREDIENTS

1 large crab
Juice $\frac{1}{2}$ lemon
2 tablespoons fresh, chopped parsley
4 tablespoons soft brown breadcrumbs
2 tablespoons mayonnaise
1 teaspoon Dijon mustard
1 hard-boiled egg, finely chopped

If you are buying the crab already cleaned, remove the white and brown meat and put into separate bowls. Now skip the next paragraph and go on to METHOD.

How to clean and prepare crab

Twist off the claws and legs, close to the body. Open the crab from the back. Get rid of the feathery, spongy-looking grey bits, known as dead man's fingers, and the little sac from behind the head. The rest of the crab is edible. Remove the white meat from the legs, the claws and the body with a fork or a pick, then scoop out all the brown meat. Put the different coloured meats into separate bowls.

METHOD

Add the lemon juice and chopped parsley to the white meat, and mix together. Add the breadcrumbs to the brown meat, together with the mayonnaise and Dijon mustard. Mix together. To serve, you can either lay the meat out on a plate, or, if you are feeling rustic, pack it back into the cleaned, washed out crab shell. Either way, the idea is to have a strip of white and green meat between two strips of brown meat. Then sprinkle a finely chopped hard-boiled egg over the top for decoration. All you then need is lots of brown bread and butter – and a little privacy!

PRAWN AND BROCCOLI GRATIN

SERVES FOUR

Broccoli used to be a luxury vegetable, now it is even more available than cauliflower. In America, apart from potatoes, it is *the* most eaten vegetable. Prawn and Broccoli Gratin is a lovely comforting dish. It is also a pretty colour, and I always think you eat with the eye as well as with the palate.

INGREDIENTS

1 lb (450 g) broccoli florets
6 oz (175 g) cooked peeled prawns
½ pt (300 ml) milk (full-fat or semi-skimmed – NOT skimmed)
1½ oz (40 g) cornflour
1 oz (25 g) butter
Alpine Salt and pepper
Pinch grated nutmeg – optional
4 oz (110 g) grated cheese – Gruyère is best, but Cheddar or Lancashire are fine

METHOD

Trim the broccoli and blanche it by dipping in boiling water for just a minute, take it out and drain. This turns it bright green but does not cook it through so, when it bakes, it stays a little crisp inside. Place the broccoli in a gratin dish – an ovenproof flat dish with sides about an inch (2.5 cm) high. Sprinkle the prawns over the broccoli. For the sauce – the Crafty white sauce which really does work a treat – put the milk, cornflour, butter, seasoning and the nutmeg all into the saucepan at once, whisk it, put it on the heat, whisk it again 2 or 3 times, not continuously, as it heats through. As it comes to the boil, give it a really thorough whisk and you will produce a wonderfully glossy white sauce without any effort – or lumps! Add the cheese and stir it in. Pour the sauce over the broccoli and prawns and bake in a medium oven, gas mark 4 / 350°F / 180°C / 160°C fan-assisted oven, or the middle of an Aga roasting oven for about 25 minutes. Do not cook it longer because the prawns will turn rubbery, or less because the broccoli will not be cooked. Serve it with granary bread – I pile it on to the granary bread and eat it like an open sandwich!

POULTRY & GAME

ROAST PHEASANT STUFFED WITH APPLES

SERVES TWO TO FOUR, DEPENDING ON THE SIZE OF THE PHEASANT

Pheasants are no longer a rare luxury. In season you can find them in most big supermarkets ready prepared. A hen bird will feed two or three people, the cock will feed four.

INGREDIENTS

1 pheasant

$1/2$ cooking apple, peeled, cored and chopped

1 sprig thyme or a teaspoon dried thyme

Alpine Salt and freshly ground black pepper

1 tablespoon redcurrant jelly

1 tablespoon double cream

METHOD

Preheat the oven to gas mark 7 / 425°F / 220°C, or 200°C fan-assisted oven. Aga users will need the top of the roasting oven. Stuff the pheasant with the apple pieces and thyme, and season generously. Wrap the breast with a piece of buttered greaseproof paper. Put it in an ovenproof casserole, put on the lid and place it in the oven for an hour. About 10 minutes before the end of the cooking time, take off the lid and remove the buttered paper. The pheasant will have cooked in its own juices and those of the apple, and will be lovely and moist. Cook it uncovered for the last 10 minutes to allow the breast to brown. When cooked, take it out and put to rest in a warm place for 5 minutes. Take the apple out of the pheasant and place in a little non-stick saucepan. Add the redcurrant jelly and double cream, and heat until the thyme-flavoured apple has completely puréed, and the redcurrant jelly and cream have mixed into it. Carve the pheasant as you would a chicken and serve some of the sauce on each plate to eat with it. Boiled potatoes and green beans or mangetout go wonderfully with this seasonal dish.

QUAIL
SERVES FOUR

Quail is one of the tiniest of the game birds. As well as being delicious, game is good for you – low in fat but with a rich taste so a little goes a long way. For each adult you need 1–2 quail. This is a way my father loved eating them, in a kind of mini-tandoori recipe.

INGREDIENTS

1–2 quail per person, 4–8 quail for four
17 fl oz (500 ml) plain yoghurt
1 tablespoon mild curry powder
1 onion
1 clove garlic
1 lemon
¼ cucumber

To make your own curry powder grind together:

1 teaspoon cumin seed
1 teaspoon turmeric
Pinch chilli powder
Pinch ground ginger
Pinch coriander
Pinch black pepper
Pinch ground cloves

METHOD

Peel and crush the garlic, peel and chop the onion and stir with the juice of the lemon into 12 fl oz (355 ml) of yoghurt. Add the curry powder. Make sure the quail are clean inside and out, give them a quick wipe, then put them into the yoghurt mixture and leave in the fridge to marinate for between 6 and 24 hours. Take them out and remove any excess yoghurt; you can leave some on but not great dollops. Put the quail on a rack over a baking tray and place in a very hot oven, gas mark 7 / 425°F / 210°C / 190°C fan-assisted oven, or the top of an Aga roasting oven for no more than 20 minutes. They should be golden on the outside and slightly sizzly. Serve them immediately on a bed of chopped lettuce with half a lemon to squeeze over each one and some warmed nan bread. For a soothing sauce, place the rest of the plain yoghurt in a small bowl and chop some cucumber into it.

Quail

Chicken Polo

CHICKEN POLO

SERVES FOUR

Chicken Polo is the Persian version of the Indian pilau. It is delicious, subtly and delicately spiced, and easy to make. If you are serving this for a dinner party use chicken breasts, otherwise you can make it with cheap chicken pieces like legs or thighs. Optional for this recipe but well worth using is saffron – the most expensive spice in the world. It costs more than its own weight in gold and a little has the effect of turning things bright gold. You only need a pinch and a little packet of saffron powder can be bought quite cheaply.

INGREDIENTS

4 chicken pieces
10 oz (275 g) long-grain rice
1 clove garlic
2 bay leaves
1 stick cinnamon
2 pods cardamom
1 oz (25 g) butter
1 fl oz (30 ml) olive oil
1 pt (600 ml) chicken stock (home-made or stock cube)
Alpine Salt
A pinch saffron – optional
A few chopped almonds

METHOD

In a large, solid frying pan heat the oil and then the butter. Finely chop the garlic and fry until pale gold – do not let it burn. Add the rice and turn it in the butter and oil until translucent. Add the bay leaves, the stick of cinnamon and the cardamom pods, and then add the chicken. Fry the rice and chicken together for about 5 minutes until the chicken is pale gold. Then add the stock. The trick of good rice is to have exactly double the quantity of liquid to rice by volume – that way the rice absorbs exactly the right amount of liquid. Then add the saffron if you are using it, and a good pinch of salt. Stir the whole thing and let it cook very gently for about 20 minutes with a cover on. The chicken cooks through in the stock. Its flavours are absorbed by the rice, the saffron turns it gold, and the garlic, bay leaves, cinnamon and cardamom flavour and scent it like a spice market. For the last 5 minutes take off the lid to make sure all the liquid is absorbed, and serve as it is on a large platter. Traditionally, almonds are sprinkled over it.

CHICKEN CHASSEUR
SERVES FOUR

In classic French cookery, *chasseur* (huntsman) in a recipe title meant there was game in it somewhere. Now it has come to mean a sautéed dish with mushrooms. This one is simple, delicious and quick.

INGREDIENTS

1 medium-sized chicken, cut into 4, or 4 chicken breasts
1/2 lb (225 g) button or chestnut mushrooms
1 large onion
1 cup chicken stock or water
4 fl oz (120 ml) double cream
1 dessertspoon cornflour
1 tablespoon each cooking oil and butter
Alpine Salt and freshly ground black pepper

METHOD

In a large frying pan or shallow saucepan, melt the butter in the oil and sauté the pieces of chicken over a medium heat until they turn golden. It will take about 5 to 6 minutes each side. Season with salt and freshly ground black pepper. Chop the onion very finely, add to the chicken and cook for a minute so the chicken and onion start to interchange flavours. Add the stock or water, check the seasoning and simmer, turning the chicken once, for about 15 minutes until it is quite cooked through. Make sure there is no pink left in the chicken. Trim the mushrooms but do not peel them. Put them in a colander and pour a kettle of boiling water over to sterilise them and get off all the dirt. Cut the mushrooms into quarters if they are quite big, and add them to the chicken and onion mixture once the chicken is cooked. Stir the cornflour into the double cream until it is smooth and add to the pan to make the sauce. You can take the chicken out and keep it warm before you do this – I do not, but that is because I am lazy! Stir it all together quickly and the sauce will thicken and absorb the juices left in the pan from the chicken stock. The cornflour thickens the sauce and you get this wonderful golden-brown coating for the chicken. Serve with rice or mashed potato or, *in extremis*, crusty French bread to mop up the juices.

CHICKEN FLORENTINE

SERVES FOUR

This is a dish which the late, great Michael Smith, who was a specialist in English food, used to enthuse over. It is light, delicate, and very simple to make – the perfect recipe for when there is lots of lovely fresh spinach in the shops.

INGREDIENTS

2 boned chicken breasts and two leg portions
1 packet fresh spinach
4 oz (110 g) Gruyère cheese or 4 oz (110 g) Gruyère and Parmesan mixed
Alpine Salt and pepper
For poaching the chicken
$\frac{1}{2}$ pt (300 ml) water
1 bay leaf
1 small onion, peeled
Good pinch Alpine Salt
For the Crafty white sauce
$\frac{1}{2}$ pt (300 ml) milk
1 oz (25 g) butter
$1\frac{1}{2}$ oz (40 g) cornflour
Pinch Alpine Salt
Pinch nutmeg – optional

METHOD

To poach the chicken, put the chicken pieces, water, bay leaf, onion and salt into a saucepan. Bring to the boil and immediately turn down the heat so it just simmers very gently for about 20 minutes. In a separate, non-stick saucepan, whisk together the milk, butter and cornflour to make the white sauce. You can add a pinch of salt and, if you like, a little pinch of nutmeg. Whisk the sauce every now again until it is thick, creamy and smooth. Rinse the spinach and plunge it into boiling water for a couple of minutes. Drain it thoroughly and chop with the back of a knife, more to get the water out than to cut it right through. Put the spinach in an ovenproof dish, and lay the poached chicken on top. Season generously, pour on the white sauce and sprinkle the grated cheese over the top. To make it extremely Florentinish, (even though they do not eat this in Florence!) mix in some grated Parmesan with the Gruyère. Place the dish under a hot grill until the cheese is bubbling. Serve so that each person gets green spinach, softly poached chicken and the creamy, cheesy sauce. Just delicious!

Top: *Chicken Florentine*   Bottom: *Chicken Provençale*

CHICKEN PROVENÇALE

SERVES FOUR

A recipe to remind you of the sun – full of colour, warmth, and a vivid, herby, jolly sort of flavour. This is a very easy, one-dish meal. It is best served with noodles – broad flat tagliatelle – as in the South of France, though you can use potatoes or rice if you prefer. Either joint a chicken – about 3 lb (1.35 kg) – or buy a couple of breasts and a couple of thighs and divide them. This means that two people are going to be OK, and two people are going to be really, really OK!

INGREDIENTS

4 pieces chicken
1 large onion, chopped
1 red pepper, de-seeded and chopped
1 clove garlic, chopped
½ litre (20 fl oz) *passata*
2 tablespoons olive oil
1 teaspoon each dried basil and oregano
Alpine Salt and pepper to taste
4 anchovy fillets – optional
6 black olives – optional

METHOD

Heat the oil in a deep frying pan, preferably with a lid. Add the chicken joints and fry over a medium heat until brown. Add the onion, pepper and garlic all chopped up, the *passata* and the herbs. Season quite generously, but not too much salt if you are going to use the anchovies and olives as they have quite a lot of salt in them. Stir, put the lid on, cook over a medium to low heat for about 25 minutes until the chicken is tender and *thoroughly* cooked through. When the chicken is ready, chop up the anchovies and stir them into the sauce. If using them, dot the olives over the top just before you serve the dish – they need nothing more than a little warming through to add their rather pungent flavour. Serve either in a great big dish surrounded by the noodles, which is my favourite thing as it looks unbelievably rich and generous, or on individual plates if you prefer.

CHICKEN PIZZAEOLA

SERVES FOUR

East of the Appenine Mountains in Italy, that is, the side facing Albania and Greece, they have a taste for slightly spicy food. It is sometimes called Arabbiatta food and has some chilli in it, dating back to the time when the Arabs and Turks variously came north and westwards, deep into Italy. This is a recipe that can be used with either steak or chicken.

INGREDIENTS

4 boneless chicken breasts
1 onion
2 cloves garlic
1 green pepper
1 red chilli pepper or a couple of shakes of chilli sauce
14-oz (400 g) tin chopped Italian tomatoes with herbs
$\frac{1}{2}$ teaspoon sugar
$\frac{1}{2}$ teaspoon lemon juice
1 teaspoon oregano
2 tablespoons olive oil
Alpine Salt and pepper

METHOD

Finely chop the garlic, onion, green pepper and chilli pepper (if you are using it). Heat a frying pan large enough to hold all the chicken pieces. It also needs a lid. Heat the oil, then add the chopped garlic and the chicken, and cook skin side down for 5 minutes. Then turn it over and cook for another couple of minutes until brown all over.

Turn the heat down and add the finely chopped onion, green pepper, and chilli pepper or a little chilli sauce. Put on the lid and let it cook quietly for about 15 minutes. It is important to let the chicken cook properly all the way through. Add the chopped tomatoes, sugar, lemon juice and oregano. Stir all round to pick up the crusty bits on the bottom and spoon over the chicken. Put the lid back on and leave over a very low heat for another 5 minutes to allow the sauce to mix and blend. Check it for seasoning, and it is ready to serve. In Italy they would not necessarily serve this with pasta; they are more likely to serve it with rice or sauté potatoes. A good green salad afterwards is the only other thing you need. It is a marvellous dish: the sauce is rich, red and spicy and sets off the mild, delicate chicken deliciously.

CHINESE CHICKEN AND PEPPERS

SERVES FOUR

This is a dish to stir-fry. It is usually made in a wok, but a large frying pan is fine, preferably non-stick. It is very, very easy to make. The secret is to get the pan very hot before you put anything in it.

INGREDIENTS

1 lb (450 g) boneless chicken meat – thighs are fine for this, breasts if you want to splash out!
1 red pepper
1 green pepper
1 Spanish onion
For the sauce
2 tablespoons soy sauce
2 tablespoons water
1 teaspoon brown sugar
1 teaspoon cornflour
1 teaspoon lemon juice

METHOD

The great trick with Chinese food is to cut everything to the same size, and to have a good, broad spatula to make the stir-frying even easier. Wash the red and green peppers, and take out the seeds and white bits inside. Peel the onion and slice into half-inch (1 cm) slices, and do the same with the peppers. Cut the chicken meat against the grain into the same sort of sized pieces. Heat the oil in the pan until it is almost smoking. Put in the chicken and fry it quickly. The pieces are quite small so it should take about 4–5 minutes. Push it to the side of the pan and add the onions and the peppers. Stir those and fry for another 3 or 4 minutes. The chicken, meanwhile, is quietly cooking on the side of the pan. In a cup stir together the soy sauce, water, brown sugar, cornflour and lemon juice. Mix until it is a really smooth mixture, then pour into the pan and toss the whole lot together. It looks a bit unpromising for the first 10 seconds, then suddenly the cornflour starts to work and the sauce goes thick and glossy and coats everything. All those wonderful colours, tastes and textures are covered in the marvellous sweet and sour sauce. Serve it immediately the sauce has thickened and gone glossy, with lots of plain boiled rice.

TOP: *Chinese Chicken and Peppers*   BOTTOM: *Discovery Chicken*

DISCOVERY CHICKEN

SERVES FOUR

I think the nicest early English apples of all are Discoveries, which are bright and beautiful, and have a light tinge of pink to them. They are called Discovery because they were 'discovered' in a clergyman's garden on what was thought to be a tree of Worcester apples. They are lovely hot, when they give off a very delicate scent. Combined with chicken, they make a delicious summery dish which, if you want to be posh about it, is a lighter version of a rich autumnal Normandy recipe called Poulet Vallée d'Auge.

INGREDIENTS

4 chicken breasts
1 tablespoon cooking oil
1 teaspoon tarragon, fresh or freeze-dried
$1/2$ pt (300 ml) apple juice
5 fl oz (150 ml) double cream
2 Discovery apples
1 oz (25 g) butter
Alpine Salt and freshly ground black pepper
$1/2$ teaspoon ground allspice

METHOD

In a large pan which will hold all 4 pieces of chicken at once, heat the oil and then sauté the chicken until it is lightly browned. Sprinkle over the tarragon and add the apple juice. Season lightly, cover the pan and simmer for about 20 minutes, turning the chicken once. Take out the chicken and put it on to a warm serving plate. Add the cream to the sauce, bring to the boil and let it bubble for 2 or 3 minutes until the sauce is reduced. The cream will thicken the sauce. (Don't let it reduce so much that you have to be sparing when you serve it as people love this sauce!) Core but do not peel the apples and cut them into 12 sections. In a separate pan, melt the butter and quickly sauté the slices of apple until they are hot but not collapsed, and sprinkle over the ground allspice. Pour the sauce over the chicken and lay the apples in a neat fan next to it, though in my family the apples are more likely to end up in a heap. Serve with lots of mashed potatoes to soak up all that wonderful sauce.

Bon appétit!

LEMON ROAST CHICKEN

SERVES FOUR

This is my favourite way of roasting a chicken. What makes it so special is that if you decide to serve it cold and let it get cool in the dish, it produces the most succulent chicken you have ever eaten! Use a free-range chicken if you can get it – most supermarkets stock them now and they are well worth the extra expense.

INGREDIENTS

1 oven-ready chicken, $3^{1}/_{2}$–4 lb (1.5–1.8 kg)

$^{1}/_{2}$ teaspoon ground bay leaves

$^{1}/_{2}$ teaspoon garlic salt

$^{1}/_{2}$ teaspoon paprika

1 lemon

METHOD

Put the chicken in an ovenproof dish into which it fits comfortably. Cut the lemon in half and put half of it inside the chicken as a stuffing. Squeeze the other half of the lemon over the chicken and then mix all the seasonings together and sprinkle over the chicken, making sure you get some on the sides as well as on the top. Grease a couple of pieces of foil with butter and loosely cover the chicken with them. Put it in an oven, gas mark 5 / 375°F / 190°C / 170°C fan-assisted oven, or the middle of an Aga roasting oven for 20 minutes per lb (450 g) plus 20 minutes. Check with a skewer in the thickest part of the thigh that the juices run clear. If at all pink, cook for another quarter of an hour and test again. To serve hot, make a delicious, pale, creamy gravy with the juices of the chicken, a little milk and a little cornflour. If you are serving it cold, let it cool in the dish. Either way, you have a succulent chicken, with the flavour of lemon permeating it and the herbs giving it that little extra zing. The skin will be crisp and golden.

CHICKEN SIMLA
SERVES FOUR

Simla was the Indian hill station where Kipling wrote so many of his stories. Whether he actually ate this particular dish I do not know, but it is distinctly Anglo-Indian in that it uses spices in a very British way; it is light, not over-spiced and very, very scrumptious! If you do not have a particularly sweet tooth, you can leave out some of the sugar.

INGREDIENTS

4 good chicken joints
1 tablespoon good mild curry powder
2 tablespoons soft brown sugar – muscovado
1 teaspoon garlic salt
6 tablespoons mango chutney
6 tablespoons water

METHOD

Put the curry powder, soft brown sugar and the garlic salt into a bowl, mix together and rub the chicken pieces with it. If you can then leave the chicken for an hour or two this gives it an even better flavour. Heat the grill as hot as you can and line the grill pan with a piece of silver foil. Grill the chicken skin side up for about 10 minutes, then turn it over and grill for another 10. Do not put the chicken too close to the heat; if you do, the outside will burn before the inside is cooked. Check the chicken with a skewer in the thickest part. If the juices are still pink, cook it longer; if clear, it is ready!

When cooked, the skin should be brown and blistered. Put the chicken on to a heated plate and pour the juices from the grill-pan into a saucepan. Add the mango chutney and the water, stir the whole lot round and bring to the boil. The sauce will be about as thick as single cream and will have both the spices and the sweetness from the chutney in it. Serve this with lots of white rice and a salad with yoghurt as a dressing. Wonderful!

CHICKEN AND LEEK PIE

SERVES FOUR

This is a very English pie, from Leicestershire. It is a wonderful way of using up left-over chicken, but you can also make it with fresh chicken. I usually make it with milk, but for a really thick sauce use double cream instead.

INGREDIENTS

6–8 oz (175–225 g) shortcrust or puff pastry
1½ lb (700 g) fresh chicken pieces
1 lb (450 g) leeks
4 eggs
2 bay leaves
Juice of half a lemon
½ pt (300 ml) milk or double cream
1 cup chicken poaching liquid or chicken stock
1½ oz (40 g) cornflour
1 oz (25 g) butter
Alpine Salt and freshly ground black pepper
Pinch grated nutmeg

METHOD

Place a little water, the lemon juice, bay leaves and chicken pieces in a saucepan. Cover and simmer until cooked – about 15 minutes. Remove the chicken, allow to cool and take the meat off the bone. (Keep the cooking liquid.) Meanwhile, put the eggs on to hard boil.

Wash the leeks thoroughly, cut into half-inch (1 cm) pieces, mix with the chicken and put them into an oval pie dish. Pour a cupful of the poaching liquid (or light chicken stock) into a saucepan, add the milk or cream and make a white sauce with the butter and flour. For the Crafty way of doing this, see page 6. Pour the sauce over the chicken and stir gently. Shell the hard-boiled eggs, cut them in half lengthways and arrange them on top. Wet the rim of the pie dish, take a little bit of the pastry, roll it into a long thin sausage and stick it round the rim. Roll out the rest of the pastry and put that on top of the pastry rim, gently smoothing the join. Make a slot in the top for the steam to come out, and brush the pastry with a little milk. Bake in a medium oven, gas mark 4 / 350°F / 180°C / 160°C fan-assisted oven, or the middle of an Aga roasting oven for 45–50 minutes until the pastry has browned and risen.

TANDOORI CHICKEN
SERVES·FOUR TO SIX

Tandoori chicken really caught on in this country about 10 years ago. Curiously, it only became widely popular in India about 10 years before that. Until then it was confined to a small part of the northern Punjab. It is very easy to make at home. The spices are readily available – you can use either a mild curry powder or a tandoori mix which you can find in most supermarkets. The only thing wrong with it is it will stain everything bright red, including your fingers. In India and Pakistan this red colouring is hardly ever used, though we seem to have come to expect it!

INGREDIENTS

1 whole chicken, cut into 6 portions
16 fl oz (480 ml) plain yoghurt
1 tablespoon mild curry powder or tandoori mix
2 cloves garlic
1 large onion
Chopped mint

METHOD

Peel and chop the onion and garlic very finely and mix in a large non-metal bowl with the yoghurt, chopped mint, and the curry or tandoori spices. Skin the chicken pieces, put them into the bowl and cover with the yoghurt and spice mix. Leave in the fridge for a minimum of 2 hours and a maximum of 24 hours. The longer you leave it the more the flavours penetrate. When you are ready to cook, heat the oven to gas mark 6 / 400°F / 200°C / 180°C fan-assisted oven, or the top of an Aga roasting oven – which, incidentally is brilliant for cooking this. Take the chicken out of the marinade, which you can now throw away, and lay the pieces on a rack so the heat can get all round (put an oven tray underneath to catch the drips!) Cook in the oven for about 30 minutes until the outside is crisp and the inside thoroughly cooked but still succulent. Put the chicken on to a plate on a bed of thinly sliced lettuce with quarters of lemon round the outside to squeeze over. Serve with hot nan bread, which again you can buy everywhere, mango chutney and a little more yoghurt to eat as a cooler. Do not bother with knives and forks – something as good as this demands just fingers and finger bowls.

PALACE RICE
SERVES FOUR

This is the Cambodian version of fried rice. Its slightly curious name is probably due to its exotic richness. Everything in this has either been pre-cooked or can be eaten raw, so although there are a lot of ingredients, it is quick to assemble and very impressive. As the cooking process is really stir-frying, a wok is ideal for this if you have one – otherwise a large frying pan or even a large, shallow saucepan.

INGREDIENTS

$1/2$ lb (225 g) cooked chicken breasts
$1/2$ lb (225 g) peeled and cooked prawns
12 oz (350 g) cooked medium- or long-grain rice
6 oz (175 g) tinned water chestnuts, sliced
4 oz (110 g) cashew nuts
4 oz (110 g) button or chestnut mushrooms
4 oz (110 g) carrots
4 oz (110 g) green peas – frozen
1 clove garlic
3 tablespoons soy sauce
2 tablespoons oil
2 eggs
Pinch Alpine Salt
Pepper to taste

METHOD

In a large frying-pan heat the oil. Peel and chop the garlic and add to the pan. Peel and slice the carrots, wipe and slice the mushrooms and add them together with the peas. Cut the chicken into chunks, add with the prawns and stir. Then add the water chestnuts and the cashew nuts, and stir again. Add the eggs and stir until it begins to form an omelette. After a minute, break the omelette up, add all the rice then stir it all together. Toss it together until the whole lot is golden and fragrant; it takes about 3–4 minutes. Sprinkle on the soy sauce, check it for seasoning and serve it in bowls. You could serve a little chicken soup with noodles to start the meal, with a dash of soy sauce.

TOP: *Palace Rice*   BOTTOM: *Classic seasoning from the Alps*

Yakitori – Japanese Kebabs

YAKITORI – JAPANESE KEBABS

SERVES FOUR

These kebabs are delicious and nutritious, and look wonderful on the long bamboo skewers you can buy in supermarkets. These are very cheap and you throw them away afterwards – so there is no danger of being skewered under the washing-up water!

INGREDIENTS

12 oz (350 g) chicken breasts
1 green pepper
4 spring onions
4 oz (110 g) small mushrooms

For the sauce
1 tablespoon caster sugar
8 tablespoons soy sauce – Japanese soy sauce if you can find it
4 teaspoons either sweet sherry, apple juice, or mirin – Japanese sweet, white rice wine for cooking
10 fl oz (300 ml) water

METHOD

You will need 8 skewers for this. Put the sugar, soy sauce, water and apple juice or sherry or mirin into a saucepan, and boil until reduced by about half. Light the grill – you need it really hot. Then prepare the kebabs. Each person has one kebab of vegetables and one of chicken. Peel and cut the onions into 1-inch (2.5 cm) pieces. Clean the seeds out of the pepper and cut that into 1-inch (2.5 cm) pieces. Trim and wash the mushrooms. Thread them on to the skewers so it goes pepper, onion, mushroom and so on, until the skewer is half full. Then cut the chicken breasts into 1-inch (2.5 cm) cubes and put those on to the skewers, and again leave half the skewer unused. Dip the kebabs into the sauce. The best way is to pour the sauce into a tall glass and dip the kebabs into that. Put the kebabs under the hot grill. Halfway through cooking – after about 4–5 minutes – take them out, dip them in the sauce again and turn them when you put them back under the grill. Cook them for another 4–5 minutes. Put the sauce back into a saucepan and boil it up again for a few minutes, then dip the kebabs in it just before serving. It gives the kebabs a lovely glistening, almost lacquered, coating – which looks even more wonderful if you lay them on a heaped bed of rice. A crisp green salad to follow is all you need.

MARMALADE DUCK

SERVES TWO

This is one of the silliest recipes you have ever met, but it works a treat! The duck for this is mallard – the breast is quite lean and wonderful, and makes the perfect meal for two. You can buy them in most good supermarkets, cleaned and ready to cook.

INGREDIENTS

1 mallard
2–3 tablespoons good chunky marmalade
Alpine Salt and pepper

METHOD

Put the marmalade in a bowl and make sure there are no really huge chunks in it. Cut them if there are and thickly spread the breast of the mallard with the marmalade as if it were toast. Put it in a roasting tin in a really hot oven, gas mark 8 / 450°F / 220°C / 200°C fan-assisted oven, or the top of an Aga roasting oven for approximately 40 minutes. If the marmalade keeps sliding off the bird, spoon it back on, but that is all you need do. When it is cooked, take it out of the oven and, with a really sharp knife, remove the breasts whole if you can and put each on to a warmed serving plate. You can use the rest of the bird for a duck salad, stock or casserole. Add a little water to the roasting tin, heat it and scrape up all the crusty bits so it forms a gravy with the marvellous bitter-sweet flavour of orange marmalade. Check the seasoning. The duck is covered with a deep golden, almost mahogany crust. Serve it with a few boiled potatoes, a crisp green vegetable, and that gravy.
It is quite wonderful, and so simple!

Dinner for two – Marmalade Duck, Carrots cooked with Star Anise, and Beans sautéed with Garlic

CHICKEN WITH LIME AND GINGER

SERVES FOUR

What makes this clear-tasting dish so easy to prepare are those boned and unskinned chicken breasts you can now buy in most supermarkets. They are very good value and repay a bit of attention to turn them into a really delicious meal.

INGREDIENTS

4 boned and unskinned chicken breasts
2 limes
1 oz (25 g) fresh peeled ginger
1 tablespoon runny honey
1 tablespoon soy sauce
Alpine Salt and freshly ground black pepper

METHOD

Put the chicken breasts into a glass or china bowl (not a metal one). Squeeze the limes and pour the juice over the chicken. Add the honey and the soy sauce. Grate the ginger and spread it over the chicken and leave to marinate in the fridge as long as possible – anything from 1 to 12 hours. Turn a couple of times. Heat the grill until it is really hot. Put the chicken under it, skin side up. Grill for 4–5 minutes, then turn over, season, and grill for another 6 or 7 minutes. If you have to, turn the heat down slightly, but make sure the chicken is cooked all the way through. Meanwhile, put the marinade into a saucepan, bring to the boil and let it bubble for a few minutes. Pour it over the chicken just before you serve. This is lovely with rice, nice with mashed potatoes, and – without the sauce – not bad in a sandwich!

TURKEY SCALLOPINI

SERVES TWO

Supermarkets really are trying hard. Turkey escalopes, available in almost all of them, are fairly new, very convenient, full of protein, low in fat, and lend themselves to all sorts of wonderful variations. This is one of my favourites.

INGREDIENTS

2 6-oz (175 g) turkey escalopes
1 glass sparkling muscatel grape juice or vermouth
5 fl oz (150 ml) double cream
Alpine Salt and pepper
1 tablespoon oil
1 tablespoon butter

METHOD

Put the escalopes on to a large piece of cling film, cover with more cling film and flatten gently with the back of a heavy frying pan to spread and really thin them. Peel off the cling film. Heat the oil, then the butter in the frying pan. Put in the meat, press it down so it is all in contact with the frying pan, count to 30, turn the turkey over, press it down and count to 30 again. The meat will be thoroughly cooked through – you do not ever want pink turkey – but very tender. Put the meat on to warmed plates. Pour the grape juice or vermouth into the frying pan, stir it round to pick up all the bits from the meat, then add the double cream and let it bubble (double cream boils beautifully) and reduce slightly. Pour it over the turkey and serve with pasta and mangetout.

SUMMER STEW
SERVES FOUR

I have been cooking and eating this since my student days. It is full of goodness, looks wonderful, and vegetables are cheap! The meat I recommend for this was not easily available in the Dark Ages when I was a student: boneless turkey thighs. Most good supermarkets now sell them pre-packed – they are very cheap, low in fat and high in flavour.

INGREDIENTS

1–1$\frac{1}{2}$ lb (450–700 g) boneless turkey thighs
2 green peppers or 1 red and 1 green pepper
1 large onion
$\frac{1}{2}$ lb (225 g) courgettes
$\frac{1}{2}$ lb (225 g) fresh or tinned Italian plum tomatoes
1 clove garlic
2 tablespoons olive oil
Good pinch fresh thyme, oregano and basil or $\frac{1}{2}$ teaspoon each of them freeze-dried
Alpine Salt and freshly ground black pepper

METHOD

Cut the turkey into 1-inch (2.5 cm) cubes. Heat the oil in a big frying pan which has a lid and fry the turkey until it is lightly brown. Cut the courgettes, the peppers and the onion into $\frac{1}{2}$ –1-inch (1–2.5 cm) pieces, crush the garlic and add them all except the courgettes to the turkey in the frying pan. Fry for 5 minutes. Chop the tomatoes, add them to the pan and season generously. Put the lid on and fry gently for 10 minutes. Add the courgettes and, if it looks a bit dry, add a little water to make some juice but not so the stew is sloshing about. Cook for another 10 minutes and, just at the end, add the fresh or freeze-dried herbs. Stir all round and serve with rice or new potatoes, or even some of that lovely fresh egg pasta. It makes a wonderful, bright, summery dish – full of colour and fresh vegetable flavours.

Summer Stew

IRISH STEW
SERVES FOUR

This is perfect comfort food, wonderful to eat when you are cold and damp. The traditional recipe used mutton but that is hard to come by now. Lamb, however, does perfectly well. The true Irish stew never, ever, uses carrots!

INGREDIENTS

1 lb (450 g) old potatoes
$^1/_2$ lb (225 g) new potatoes
1$^1/_2$ lb (700 g) lamb or mutton chops
1 lb (450 g) onions
Alpine Salt and pepper

METHOD

Wash and scrub the new potatoes, but do not peel them. They should be quite small, about the size of half an egg. Peel the old potatoes and the onions, and cut both into thick slices. Line the bottom of a nice big casserole with a layer of sliced potato, then a layer of onion, then a layer of chops, using about half the quantity of each. Season generously with salt and pepper. On top of that put another layer of sliced potato, a layer of onion and the rest of the chops, and then on top arrange the washed and scrubbed new potatoes. Season generously and just cover with water. Cook in a medium oven, gas mark 4 / 350°F / 180°C / 160°C fan-assisted oven, or the middle of an Aga roasting oven for about an hour to an hour and a half, depending on the size and age of the chops. Mutton will need a good hour and a half. The potato at the bottom will cook almost to a purée, the potato at the top will stay firm, so make sure everyone gets some soft potato, some firm potato, some chops and onion. The only way to eat this is in a bowl, sprinkled with chopped parsley.

LAMB SATÉ
SERVES SIX

Saté consists of meat, prawns, chicken or vegetarian chunks on a stick and comes from South-East Asia. The key thing is this wonderful, wonderful sauce which is fundamentally exotic peanut butter.

INGREDIENTS

1½ lb (700 g) boneless lamb, cut into small cubes
1 medium-sized onion, finely chopped
1 clove garlic, finely chopped
1 tablespoon each soft brown sugar and soy sauce
1 teaspoon each ground coriander and ground ginger
Juice of a lemon
4 tablespoons peanut butter – preferably crunchy
1 cup water

METHOD

You need long skewers for this, bamboo or metal (6 or 12). Put the cubed lamb into a large bowl – NOT a metal one – and add the rest of the ingredients as a marinade except the peanut butter and water. Mix well to make sure the lamb is coated, then leave in the fridge for up to 12 hours. When you are ready to cook, thread the lamb on to the skewers, leaving a long handle, and place them under a hot grill, turning so they are browned on all sides and cooked through. Meanwhile, put the peanut butter and water into a saucepan, add the remaining marinade and bring to the boil. It looks dreadful. But suddenly it turns into a smooth, glossy, chocolate-looking sauce, full of flavour. Pour it over the saté and serve with rice and a crisp green salad.

ROAST LAMB
SERVES FOUR

You can use either shoulder or leg for this. The main difference is that shoulder is cheaper, but also a bit fattier. I often buy shoulder and cut off some of the extraneous fat. Do not buy anything smaller than 3–4 lb, the meat shrinks so much it vanishes!

INGREDIENTS

3–4 lb (1.35–1.8 kg) leg (or shoulder) of lamb
1 teaspoon rosemary
½ teaspoon ground bay leaves
Pinch Alpine Salt and pepper
1 pt (600 ml) water, to go in roasting dish
Cornflour – optional

METHOD

Use a roasting dish with a rack that will sit above the water. Rub the lamb all over with the rosemary, ground bay and seasoning. Put it on the rack over the water, and place in a very hot oven, gas mark 7 / 425°F / 210°C / 190°C fan-assisted oven, or the top of an Aga roasting oven. Roast for 15 minutes to the pound (450 g) if you like the lamb pink, 18 minutes to the pound (450 g) if you like it medium, and 25 minutes to the pound (450 g) if you like it ruined! Take it out of the oven. It will be lovely and crisp on the outside, moist on the inside, and the water will have made the gravy. The liquid will have reduced to about half a pint (300 ml). You can thicken it with cornflour or even a gravy browning. It has the flavour of the lamb and herbs, and if you reduce it further becomes that wonderful, pure, shiny *jus* beloved of the French. Wrap the lamb loosely in foil and leave to stand for about 15 minutes. It will slice like butter and taste wonderful.

LAMB KLEFTIKO

SERVES FOUR

Lamb Kleftiko is a wonderful, melting baked dish from rural Greece. *Kleftiko* and *klepto* (as in mania) have the same root; the recipe gets its name from sheep-stealers who cooked the sheep to make quite sure the rightful owners never got them back! Apart from being warming and delicious, this dish works best with one of the cheaper cuts of lamb.

INGREDIENTS

1 shank end of leg or shoulder of lamb
1 clove garlic
1 onion
6 medium tomatoes
6 medium potatoes
1 teaspoon dried rosemary or sprig fresh rosemary
Alpine Salt and pepper

METHOD

Peel and chop the garlic and onion. If the lamb is fatty, trim the fat. Put the lamb into a casserole into which it fits comfortably. Sprinkle over it the garlic and onion, and add the rosemary. Cut the tomatoes into quarters and put them in as well. Cover the casserole and bake it very gently in a low to moderate oven, gas mark 3 / 325°F / 170°C / 150°C fan-assisted oven, or the lower oven of an Aga. Cook it for about 45 minutes to an hour. Meanwhile, peel or scrub the potatoes, and cut them into walnut-sized pieces. Add the potatoes to the casserole dish, turn them in the juices, season generously with salt and pepper and cook for another 45 minutes to an hour until the potatoes are cooked through. The potatoes will absorb the most wonderful flavours and juices. The meat will be so soft you can almost cut if off the bone with a spoon, and the juices, onions and tomatoes will all have amalgamated to make a lovely rich, herby sauce. Serve with crusty bread, preferably Greek bread with sesame seeds on it which you have first warmed in the oven.

Lamb Kleftiko and Champ

Lamb Saté and Sasatis

SASATIS
SERVES FOUR

This is a super dish for a barbecue, but can just as easily be cooked indoors and then eaten outside, which I have to say is my preferred combination! It is a kebab recipe from South Africa. Sasatis are delicious; they are slightly curried and cooked with apricots.

INGREDIENTS

1 lb (450 g) boned leg, shoulder or fillets of lean lamb
8 oz (225 g) fresh or 4 oz (110 g) dried apricots
1 onion, peeled and chopped
2 tablespoons oil
1 dessertspoon mild curry powder
$1/2$ teaspoon Alpine Salt – Alpine Herb Salt is nice in this
Juice of a lemon
2 bay leaves

METHOD

If you are using dried apricots, soak them in water, orange juice or cold tea (delicious!) for a couple of hours. If the apricots are fresh, take out the stones. Heat the oil in a saucepan and fry the onion gently until it is translucent. Add the curry powder and fry gently for a couple of minutes until the smell is fragrant. Add the apricots – if you are using dried apricots, add some of the liquid they were soaked in as well – and cook for a couple of minutes. Add the salt, the juice of a lemon and the bay leaves, and either liquidise or put in a food processor. It should produce a purée about the thickness of double cream. If you need to, add a little more of the apricot soaking liquid. Cut the lamb into cubes and marinate it in the mixture for anything from 1 hour to 24 in the fridge, turning occasionally. The flavour just gets better and better. Put the meat on to 4 skewers and bunch it up to the sharp end so you have plenty of handle for turning it. Cook either on a barbecue or under a hot grill for about 4–5 minutes a side. It is meant to be brown on the outside but still fairly tender inside. Meanwhile, put the marinade into a saucepan, bring it to the boil for a few minutes and use it as a sauce to serve with the meat. Traditionally this is eaten with rice, though I like to eat it – one of the nicest kebabs in the world – with warmed nan bread.

VENETIAN LIVER
SERVES FOUR

The great thing about liver is that it needs only to be cooked very lightly. This is the Venetian version of liver and onions and is a great excuse to use the wonderful dark brown Balsamic vinegar from Modena in Italy. This is not cheap but you need only use small quantities. It is available now in most big supermarkets and is worth every penny. Lamb's liver does very well for this recipe, provided it is sliced really thinly. If you want to use calf's liver, as in the original recipe, it will cost you about three times as much!

INGREDIENTS

1–1½ lb (450–700 g) lamb's liver, sliced really thinly
1½ lb (700 g) onions
3 tablespoons olive oil
3 tablespoons white wine vinegar *or* 1 tablespoon Balsamic vinegar and 2 tablespoons white wine vinegar
Alpine Salt and pepper

METHOD

Peel and cut the onions in half and slice really thinly – the slicing blade on a food processor is ideal for this. In a large frying pan, heat the olive oil, put in the onions and stir. What looked like a huge mound of onions will go down a lot. Cook them for 15 minutes until they are golden brown. Season if necessary, remove the onions from the frying pan and keep warm. Now fry the liver. Put the slices into the frying pan in a single layer so they do not overlap and add the vinegar. Allow no more than 30 seconds each side. If you cook liver for more than that, you might as well not bother; if you cook it really fast it stays just that tiny bit pink in the middle, and delicate and delicious. As soon as the second side has had its 30 seconds, take the liver out and put it on top of the onions. Pour the pan juices, which are now sweet and sour from the aromatic caramelisation of the onions and the distillation of the vinegar, over the lot. Serve extremely quickly. Eaten at the moment of perfection it is one of the most delicious dishes imaginable.

CUTLETS MILANESE
SERVES FOUR

This is a very simple way of making lamb chops different. You can use ordinary English chops, but also available now are really thin chops, only about half an inch (1 cm) thick, which are very cheap and good value. Properly speaking they are cutlets and perfect for this.

INGREDIENTS

8 ordinary lamb chops or 16 thin cutlets
1 egg
2 slices white bread
4 oz hard dry cheese – old mousetrap from the back of the fridge will do, Parmesan is better
1 teaspoon oregano
A little olive oil
Alpine Salt and pepper

METHOD

Beat the egg, turn the bread into crumbs – a quick whizz in a food processor is the easiest method – and grate the cheese. Mix the grated cheese and breadcrumbs together, and season. Dip the chops or cutlets into the beaten egg and then into the breadcrumb and cheese mixture, making sure they are well coated. Sprinkle each one with a little oregano. When you have done them all, fry them in the olive oil in a big pan; if you do not have one large enough to hold all the meat you may have to use two. If you are cooking the very thin cutlets, they take about 5 minutes – $3^1/_2$ minutes on one side, $1^1/_2$ on the other. The chops take about another 2 minutes on one side, 1 minute on the other. Do not cook them too long; you want them brown on the outside but still succulent on the inside, not like shoe leather. As soon as they are cooked, take them quickly out of the pan, drain them on a bit of kitchen paper and serve straight away – they do not benefit from hanging about. They should have a marvellous crisp coating and be tender inside. You can serve them with new potatoes and, as they are Cutlets Milanese, with a little garlic mayonnaise as well!

Cutlets Milanese

HEREFORD-SHIRE BAKE
SERVES FOUR

This is one of the nicest supper dishes I know – cheap, warm, filling and quite delicious. Hereford is famous for its beef and apples, hence the name and the ingredients.

INGREDIENTS

1 lb (450 g) good beef sausages
½ lb (225 g) carrots
½ lb (225 g) onions
½ lb (225 g) cooking apples, cored – not peeled
1 tablespoon oil for frying
1 tablespoon plain flour
1 teaspoon ground sage
½ pt (300 ml) apple juice
Alpine Salt and pepper to taste

METHOD

Use a casserole that can go both on the top of the stove and in the oven. Peel and slice the carrots and onions, and slice the apples – the skin adds colour and flavour. Lightly fry the sausages in the oil in the casserole until brown. At this stage you are just browning, not cooking them. Remove the sausages and keep warm; put the apples, onion and carrots into the casserole. Fry them until they are just starting to brown. Mix in the tablespoon of flour, then add the apple juice and stir until you have a nice thick sauce. Then back in with the sausages, sprinkle in the sage, and season with salt and pepper. Put into a medium oven, gas mark 4 / 350°F / 180°C / 160°C fan-assisted oven, or the bottom of an Aga roasting oven for about 40–45 minutes until the vegetables are lusciously soft and the sausages cooked. Serve with crispy green cabbage. Wonderful!

KIDNEYS IN MUSTARD AND CREAM SAUCE
SERVES FOUR

This recipe comes from one of the gentlemen's clubs in St James's, where they used to serve it for breakfast in the 1890s. I prefer it for lunch or dinner!

INGREDIENTS

8 lamb's kidneys, trimmed
4 oz (110 g) sliced button mushrooms
5 fl oz (150 ml) double cream or fromage frais with 8% fat
1 tablespoon oil
1 oz (25 g) butter
1 tablespoon Dijon mustard
Alpine Salt and freshly ground black pepper

METHOD

Cut the kidneys in half lengthways so they look like half a butterfly. In a frying pan heat the oil then add the butter. Sauté the kidneys briskly for 3 minutes. Add the mushrooms, turn them with the kidneys, and season with salt and pepper. Pour in all the cream or fromage frais and stir. The mixture will pick up all the lovely golden bits from the pan and begin to thicken slightly. Double cream will not curdle, separate or do anything nasty when it is heated. You can even boil it. Fromage frais is not so accommodating – see Infallible Hints, page 7. Then add the mustard and stir until well blended in. The sauce will turn a rich golden colour. Check for seasoning and serve with as much mashed potato as you dare eat, and something crisp and green – beans, mangetout, or crisply cooked cabbage.

MEAT LOAF
SERVES FOUR

This is the ultimate basic minced-beef meat loaf, and one of my favourite dishes. It is very cheap to make and most enjoyable to eat.

INGREDIENTS

1 lb (450 g) lean minced beef
1 large onion, finely chopped
2 slices bread – wholemeal or white
1 egg
$^1/_2$ cup milk
Alpine Salt and pepper
$^1/_2$ teaspoon each thyme, marjoram, rosemary

METHOD

Put the mince into a bowl and mix in the onion. Put the bread into another bowl, add the milk and mix together until the bread has absorbed the milk. Spoon this mixture into the mince and add all the seasonings, herbs and the egg, and mix in with the mince. There is no way round this: you have to roll up your sleeves and squelch it. When mixed, it should be moist but coherent. Press into a 2-lb (1 kg) loaf tin, then turn it upside-down on to a baking sheet and remove the tin. Place the meat loaf in a medium oven, gas mark 4 / 350°F / 180°C / 160°C fan-assisted oven, or the bottom of an Aga roasting oven and roast for about 45–50 minutes. Slice it nice and thickly like a loaf, and serve with lots of mashed potato, crispy cooked cabbage, and perhaps some glazed carrots cooked with a pinch of sugar and a knob of butter.

ITALIAN MEATBALLS (POLPETTE) AND TOMATO SAUCE
SERVES FOUR

In Italy *polpette* comes in all kinds and varieties, shapes and sizes. This is a very simple recipe that can equally well be comfort food or a splendid dinner-party dish.

ITALIAN MEATBALLS

INGREDIENTS

1 lb (450 g) lean minced beef
2 slices wholemeal bread
1 onion, finely chopped
2 cloves garlic, finely chopped
1 egg
1 teaspoon oregano
1 dessertspoon olive oil
Alpine Salt and pepper
17 fl oz (500 ml) tomato sauce, preferably home-made (see right)

METHOD

You need a nice big bowl and very clean hands. Put the wholemeal bread into the bowl and moisten with a little water. Add the beef, onion, garlic, egg, oregano and seasoning, and squelch it all about a bit until well blended (this is why you need clean hands!). Divide the mixture into 16 bits – do not guess – halve it first, then quarter it and so on. It takes no longer and your meatballs all end up the same size. Roll each piece between the wetted palms of your hands until it is a little ball. Heat the oil in a large frying pan, and fry the meatballs gently for about 15 minutes until they are brown all over. Then pour the tomato sauce over the meatballs and simmer for another 5–10 minutes so the flavours blend. Check for seasoning and serve with lots of tagliatelle, the flat Italian pasta, grated Parmesan, and a little freshly ground black pepper.

TOMATO SAUCE

INGREDIENTS

20 fl oz (500 ml) *passata*
4 sticks celery, finely chopped
1/2 onion, finely chopped
1 carrot, grated
1 clove garlic, finely chopped
2 tablespoons olive oil
1/2 teaspoon each oregano, thyme and basil
Alpine Salt and freshly ground black pepper

METHOD

Heat the oil in a large saucepan and gently fry the vegetables and garlic for 3 minutes. Add the *passata* (a smooth tomato purée), bring to the boil and simmer gently for 20 minutes. Add the herbs and seasonings, stir well, and serve with Italian meatballs, meat loaf or just plain pasta.

TOP: *Italian Meatballs* (Polpette) *and Tomato Sauce* BOTTOM: *Beef Piquante*

BEEF PIQUANTE

SERVES FOUR

This is an adaptation of the sauté technique of cooking, used a lot in France for domestic cookery but not very much here. It is beef cooked in a sweet and sour, sharp little sauce – not swishing about in it like a casserole, but cooked quite quickly and simply. You need good beef, and that means steak. You can sometimes buy stir-fry strips, which are tender off-cuts of the rather more expensive kinds of beef, and these fit the recipe perfectly.

INGREDIENTS

1 lb (450 g) stir-fry beef or sirloin or rump steak
1 onion
1 clove garlic
5–6 fl oz (150–180 ml) fresh orange juice
1 tablespoon tomato purée
1 green pepper
1 tablespoon oil (NOT olive oil)
1 tablespoon butter
Pinch Alpine Salt and freshly ground black pepper
A little chilli powder or chilli sauce – optional

METHOD

If you are not using the stir-fry beef, slice the steak thinly across the grain and trim off any surplus fat. In a large frying pan, heat the oil and butter together until the butter foams. Put in the beef slices. While they are browning, peel and very finely chop the onion and garlic. When the beef is brown on both sides, add the onion and garlic, turn the heat down and let them cook very gently with the beef for 4 or 5 minutes until they are translucent and cooked through. Add the orange juice and tomato purée and stir thoroughly. The tomato purée thickens the sauce as well as giving it flavour and colour. Add the salt and pepper. If you like your food spicy, you can add a pinch of chilli powder or a few drops of chilli sauce at this point. (Surprisingly enough, the French often do.) Chop the green pepper very finely and, when the orange and tomato sauce has cooked for 5 minutes, add the pepper and cook for a further 5 minutes, so the whole thing has only cooked for 15–16 minutes. It is, after all, steak that you are cooking and does not need a long time. You will now have a very pretty orangey-pink sauce, with the little green pepper pieces studding it and the brown beef looking very savoury. Serve with lots of rice and a green salad to follow – any other vegetable will be massacred by the sauce!

BEEF COBBLER

SERVES FOUR

This is a modern version of boiled beef and carrots with dumplings. It is called cobbler because the wholemeal scone mixture is cut into rounds and put on top of the stew to look like the heels that cobblers used to keep in rows when they were mending shoes!

INGREDIENTS

For the beef stew

1$^{1}/_{2}$ lb (700 g) stewing steak

1 lb (450 g) carrots

1 large onion

Pinch herbs – marjoram and thyme are best

Good pinch Alpine Salt and black pepper

1 tablespoon oil to fry the meat

For the scone topping

4 oz (110 g) self-raising wholemeal flour *or* plain wholemeal flour and 1 tsp baking powder

2 oz (50 g) butter

2 fl oz (55 ml) milk

Good pinch Alpine Salt

METHOD

Cut the meat into walnut-sized pieces and fry in the oil in a pan until lightly browned. Peel and chop the onion, and cut the carrots into chunks about an inch (2.5 cm) long. Turn the vegetables with the meat in the pan for a moment and put into an oven-proof casserole or pie dish. Mix in the herbs and seasoning. Add just enough water to cover the meat. Put in a medium oven, gas mark 4 / 350°F / 180°C / 160°C fan-assisted oven, or the bottom of an Aga roasting oven. Let it cook uncovered for about 45 minutes – more if the meat is tough – until the meat has started to cook thoroughly. Mix together all the scone ingredients to make a fairly stiff mixture but one which can be rolled out. If too stiff to work with and a bit crumbly, add a little more milk. Roll out to about half an inch (1 cm) thick and use a cutter or glass to cut rounds about 2 inches (5 cm) wide. Carefully lay the scones on top of the meat in overlapping rows. Return the dish to the oven for another 45 minutes. The scones will rise to provide a lovely brown topping which absorbs juice from the stew. Serve with new potatoes and something green like cabbage.

CABBAGE ROLLS

SERVES FOUR

This is lovely, economical and filling. It is Middle European and very much a family dish for the middle of the week. Depending on the amount of meat you put in each cabbage leaf, this recipe will make up to 14 rolls. Do not try to make more, there will not be enough meat in them; and do not make fewer than 8, they will be too big. In fact 10 or 12 is just right!

INGREDIENTS

1 large loose-leafed green cabbage
1 lb (450 g) lean, fine-ground minced beef
1 clove garlic and 1 large onion, finely chopped
$1/2$ teaspoon allspice
1 crumbled bay leaf or a pinch ground bay leaf
1 teaspoon thyme
Alpine Salt and freshly ground black pepper
1 litre ($1^3/4$ pt) *passata* – smooth tomato purée

METHOD

Separate out the leaves of the cabbage. Put the rough, tough outer leaves to one side – you will need them later. Select about 12 large but malleable leaves. Dip them in boiling water in a big saucepan a few times until they soften so they can be rolled easily. You may need to cut off the thick bit of the stalk. Mix the beef in with the onion and garlic and the allspice, bay leaf, thyme and plenty of salt and black pepper. Then roll up your sleeves and knead it thoroughly until it is what folk in my trade call a coherent mass – or nicely mixed together! Put about one-twelfth of the meat mixture – about a tablespoon – on the bottom third of each cabbage leaf, roll it over once, fold the sides in and then keep rolling until you have a neat cigar-shaped parcel. Put the washed, rough outer leaves in the bottom of a baking dish as a base, and put the 12 (or however many you have made) cabbage rolls in nice neat rows on top. Mix a little salt and pepper into the *passata* and pour that over the cabbage rolls. Put it to bake in a medium oven, gas mark 4 / 350°F / 180°C / 160°C fan-assisted oven, or the middle of an Aga roasting oven for about 45–50 minutes. Quite a lot of the sauce is absorbed while it cooks and keeps the cabbage rolls moist. Serve the cabbage rolls with a spoonful of the sauce to each plate. Throw away the rough outer leaves. This is smashing with rice, all right with pasta, nice with mashed potato, and you do not need another vegetable.

Cabbage Rolls – before and after

BOEUF STROGANOFF

SERVES FOUR

Stroganoff is supposed to have been a Russian Count, a patron of the arts who liked everything cooked with soured cream. His French chef may well have obliged him in this. If the truth be told, the dish is a kind of Slavic stir-fry with soured cream dolloped in at the end. It is really very easy and quick to make. You need quite tender beef, and can now buy beef pre-cut for stir-fry. You can also use sirloin or rump steak.

INGREDIENTS

1 lb (450 g) beef
1 red and 1 green pepper, de-seeded
4 oz (110 g) button mushrooms
6 spring onions
8 fl oz (240 ml) soured cream
2 tablespoons oil
Alpine Salt and black pepper

METHOD

If the beef is not already prepared, cut it into ribbons about a quarter of an inch (5 mm) thick, across the grain. Wash and de-seed the peppers, and slice. Wash, trim and cut the spring onions in half lengthways, then cut into 2-inch (5 cm) lengths. Pour boiling water over the button mushrooms to clean them, and slice into quarters or more if they are quite big buttons. Heat the oil in a big, non-stick frying pan. When it is quite hot, add the beef and let it brown very quickly, in about 3 or 4 minutes. Add the peppers, mushrooms and spring onions, and turn them all together with the beef for another 4 or 5 minutes, just like a Chinese stir-fry. Season generously with the salt and pepper, and then add the soured cream. Bring it all to the boil, turning a couple of times so the cream picks up all the lovely brown crusty bits in the pan. Traditionally it is served with broad noodles – tagliatelle. If you buy fresh pasta, which cooks in just 4 minutes, from a standing start you could have this meal on the table in 12–15 minutes. A real convenience food!

TOAD IN THE HOLE WITH ONION GRAVY
SERVES FOUR

Made with classy sausages this is quite delicious. Served with Onion Gravy it is wonderful!

INGREDIENTS

1 lb (450 g) of the best sausages you can find
$^1/_2$ lb (225 g) self-raising flour
2 eggs
$^1/_2$ pt (300 ml) milk
Good pinch Alpine Salt
1 teaspoon English mustard powder

METHOD

Heat the oven to gas mark 6 / 400°F / 200°C / 180°C fan-assisted oven, or use the top of an Aga roasting oven. Place the sausages in a smallish baking tray, and bake for 5–10 minutes until the fat runs out and they begin to brown. If you plan to make onion gravy, pour off some of the fat and keep it to one side. Mix the eggs, milk, salt, mustard powder and flour together, and whisk thoroughly. Pour this batter into the hot tin on top of the sausages. Push the sausages into a tidy pattern and put it back into the oven for between 20 and 30 minutes. Keep an eye on it. The sausages will continue to cook, and the pudding should rise spectacularly. When brown and golden and crisp on the outside, it is ready.

ONION GRAVY

INGREDIENTS

1 large or 2 small onions
A little fat from the sausages or dripping
1 tablespoon flour
$^1/_2$ pt (300 ml) liquid – vegetable water or stock
Alpine Salt and pepper

METHOD

Slice the onions and cook them in the fat until they are pale gold. Add a tablespoon of flour and stir around until pale gold as well. Add the liquid. Bring to the boil while stirring gently, season to taste and there you have a lovely pale golden gravy. You could add a little Worcestershire sauce to give a slight piquancy.

STEAK PIZZAEOLA
SERVES FOUR

This comes from the same part of Italy as Chicken Pizzaeola, from that lovely, rather remote part east of the Appenines and off the normal tourist routes. One of the great benefits of a sauce like this is that you can use slightly smaller steaks!

INGREDIENTS

4 6-oz (175 g) sirloin or rump steaks
4 oz (110 g) chopped tinned tomatoes
1 tablespoon pesto sauce – ready-made from a supermarket is fine
1 clove garlic
A few drops chilli sauce
Alpine Salt and freshly ground black pepper

METHOD

Heat the grill for at least 5 minutes before putting on the steaks. Mix together the tinned tomatoes, pesto sauce, finely chopped clove of garlic and few drops of chilli sauce. When the grill is really hot, cook the steaks for 2 minutes on one side. Turn over, season with salt and pepper, and spread a quarter of the mixture on each. Put them back under the grill and cook for another 2 minutes for rare, 3 minutes for medium – and 4 minutes for ruined! And that is it. I suggest you serve the steaks with soft Italian noodles and a green salad to follow. The flavours are intense.

HUNGARIAN GOULASH
SERVES FOUR

This is one of my favourite stews – filling, warming, and simple to cook. It has been around for about a thousand years, dating back to the time of nomadic tribes which roamed the pre-Hungarian plains.

INGREDIENTS

2 lb (1 kg) lean stewing beef
2 large onions
4 tablespoons tomato purée
1 tablespoon oil
1 tablespoon paprika
1½ lb (700 g) potatoes
1 teaspoon caraway seeds
Alpine Salt and freshly ground black pepper
1 teaspoon cornflour

METHOD

Put the oil into a large ovenproof casserole, which you can also put on direct heat. Cut the beef into cubes about an inch (2.5 cm) across and brown them in the oil. Slice the onions thinly and add. Then add the tomato purée, paprika, caraway seeds, seasonings, and enough water to cover. Cook for half an hour in a medium oven, gas mark 4 / 350°F / 180°C / 160°C fan-assisted oven, or the bottom of an Aga roasting oven. Peel the potatoes and cut them into chunks. Take out the casserole, add the potatoes and cook in the oven for another 25 minutes. Mix the cornflour with a little water, stir it into the goulash and put the casserole on to the hob for about a minute, stirring gently until the whole lot thickens. Serve it with noodles and sour cream. It is the most warming and comforting of dishes!

Top: *Steak Pizzaeola*   Bottom: *Classic seasoning from the Alps*

LIVER AND ORANGE
SERVES FOUR

This is so incredibly quick and easy, you must cook the vegetables first – new potatoes and courgettes are perfect with this. You can use either lamb's or calf's liver, but beware the price of calf's liver!

INGREDIENTS

1 lb (450 g) liver, neatly and thinly sliced

1 tablespoon each oil and butter

1 small cup high-juice orange squash

1 tablespoon Worcestershire sauce

METHOD

Heat a big, solid, non-stick frying pan until it is very hot, then put in the oil. When that is hot, add the butter and let it sizzle until it stops fizzing. Put the thin slices of liver into it in one layer, so they do not overlap. Allow them 30 seconds only. Turn the liver over and pour on the undiluted orange squash – it gives a wonderful sweet-and-sour orange flavour. Add the Worcestershire sauce. Cook for another 45–50 seconds, shaking the pan, then remove the liver immediately to hot plates. Do not cook it longer or you will have orange-flavoured shoe leather. Cooked as suggested here, it will still be just pink in the middle. Another 10 seconds and it will be cooked through, but do not cook it longer than that. Pour the wonderful dark golden, glazy juices all over the liver, and eat immediately.

PASTA CARBONARA
SERVES FOUR

This is one of my favourite pasta dishes and is effortlessly easy to make. It is supposed to be a version of the pasta Italian charcoal-burners – the *carbonari* – cooked in the woods over their fires, and has a lovely, creamy, fresh taste. I use dried rather than fresh pasta for this, and the whole thing takes just 10 minutes to cook.

INGREDIENTS

12 oz (350 g) pasta

2 large eggs

3–4 tablespoons single cream

2 oz (50 g) each salami and grated Parmesan

Alpine Salt and freshly ground black pepper

METHOD

Bring a large saucepan of water to the boil and add a pinch of salt and a little oil. Drop in the pasta. Cook for 3 minutes, take off the heat, put the lid on and leave to one side. Cut the salami into matchstick-sized pieces, put them in a separate saucepan and fry them in their own fat for a minute or two until slightly crisp. Beat the cream and eggs together in a bowl. Seven minutes after you placed the lid on the pasta and put it aside, drain it. It will be perfectly cooked *al dente*. Put the pasta into a big, warmed bowl, and on top of it pour the mixed eggs and cream, and stir them around. The heat from the pasta will cook the eggs and form a wonderful, thick, creamy sauce. Put the salami on top of that and mix again. Check the seasoning and serve with Parmesan cheese and plenty of black pepper.

VEGETABLE & VEGETARIAN DISHES

CHILLI SIN CARNE
SERVES FOUR

This, as you can see from the name, is chilli without meat; what you use instead are red kidney beans. You can either buy these tinned and ready to eat, or dried, which need lengthy, but essential, soaking. Simply from the point of view of time, I recommend the tins!

INGREDIENTS

2 lb (1 kg) tinned red kidney beans
1 large onion
2 cloves garlic
1–2 tablespoons corn oil
1/2 lb (225 g) tin chopped Italian tomatoes
1/2 teaspoon each cinnamon and cumin
Chilli to taste – fresh, dried, powdered or sauce
Alpine Salt and freshly ground black pepper
1/2 lb (225 g) long-grain rice
1/2 lb (225 g) frozen sweetcorn kernels
1/2 lb (225 g) lima beans or tinned butter beans

METHOD

Peel and chop the garlic and onion, and fry them in a large pan in the oil until they are soft and golden. Drain the kidney beans and rinse off the remnants of the liquid – it contains a lot of sugar. Add them to the garlic and onions, together with the tinned tomatoes, spices and as much chilli as suits you. Start with a teaspoonful, cover and cook it all very gently for half an hour. You will only discover how powerful the chilli is once it has had a chance to blend with the other flavours. Check the seasoning. Cook the rice as you would normally. In yet another saucepan, mix together the lima or butter beans and sweetcorn kernels, add a knob of butter and heat through until they are hot but still have a bite to them. To serve, arrange the rice on 4 plates with the Chilli sin Carne on one side and the lima/butter beans and sweetcorn on the other. You have there a perfectly balanced meal, with plenty of fibre, protein, vitamins, and minerals. It also tastes pretty good!

Chilli sin Carne

Dutch Savoury Pancake

DUTCH SAVOURY PANCAKE

SERVES FOUR

This is a solid, very serious pancake with the quality of an omelette about it. White flour is best for this, though you could use wholemeal.

INGREDIENTS

For the pancake

6 oz (175 g) plain flour

2 eggs

1 teaspoon oil

For the filling

1 tablespoon oil

1 oz (25 g) butter

1 small onion

4 oz (110 g) mushrooms

4 oz (110 g) peas – frozen are fine

4 oz (110 g) cheese – Gouda or Edam are best

1 small red pepper

Alpine Salt and black pepper

METHOD

Beat the flour, eggs and teaspoon of oil together. Then beat in enough water to make a batter the consistency of single cream. When smooth, put it to one side – in the fridge if you like – for up to 2 hours. Finely chop the onion and red pepper, slice the mushrooms and chop up the cheese. Take a large frying pan, 10–12 inches (25–30 cm) in diameter, and heat the tablespoon of oil and the butter until the butter stops sizzling. Add the onion and red pepper (and the peas if you are using fresh ones), and stir until the vegetables begin to soften and the onion becomes translucent. Light the grill as you will need it well heated. Give the batter a stir, then pour it into the frying pan with the vegetables. Add the frozen peas if you are using them, the sliced mushrooms and the cheese, season generously and press the cheese and vegetables into the pancake mixture. Cook over a very gentle heat for 4–5 minutes. Put the frying pan under the hot grill for about a minute, until the top becomes golden brown and just a little crusty. Serve it straight from the pan in wedges, like a cake. It is quite thick – at least half an inch (1 cm). I eat it with just a green salad as anything else is too substantial. It is remarkably filling and quite delicious.

GRATIN OF WINTER VEGETABLES
SERVES FOUR

This can be eaten as a vegetarian dish on its own, or with sausages or grilled meats, with which it is particularly good as it has a nice rich sauce. A *gratin*, by the way, gets its name from the delicious crusty burnt bits which stick to the lid of the cooking dish and used to be scraped off and eaten (from the French *gratter*, to scrape).

INGREDIENTS

¹/₂ pt (300 ml) milk (not skimmed)
1¹/₂ oz (40 g) cornflour
1 oz (25 g) butter
Alpine Salt and freshly ground black pepper
Grated nutmeg – optional
¹/₂ lb (225 g) each leeks, carrots and parsnips
4 oz (110 g) grated cheese – Gruyère or Cheddar
4 oz (110 g) fresh breadcrumbs

METHOD

Make the white sauce first. Use a non-stick saucepan and a good whisk. Put in the milk, butter and flour, and whisk together. Heat until it goes thick, whisking every now again – do not walk away and answer the phone – then add a good pinch of salt (and nutmeg, if your are using it), and pepper. Whisk it again and put to one side.

You now have a thick, creamy, shiny white sauce. Prepare the vegetables. Peel the carrots and parsnips, wash the leeks carefully and cut them all into 1-inch (2.5 cm) chunks. Bring a big saucepan of salted water to the boil. Put all the vegetables in together and boil them for just 5 minutes. You are not softening them, just blanching them. Drain the vegetables and put them into a gratin or baking dish – anything that is round, square or oval with a flat bottom and about an inch and a half (4 cm) deep. Pour the white sauce over them and sprinkle on the grated cheese and breadcrumbs. Put it either under a grill (but not too close to the heat) for about 10 minutes, or into a hot oven, gas mark 6 / 400°F / 200°C / 180°C fan-assisted oven, or the top of an Aga roasting oven for approximately 20 minutes until the top is bubbling and golden. This dish is succulent and gorgeous – the leeks are green, the parsnips give sweetness and the carrots give crunch. I actually like it as a main course, served with wholemeal bread and butter, but you can serve it as a splendid side dish.

*Dishes from left to right: Stir-tossed Cabbage, Beans sautéed with Garlic, and Carrots cooked with
Star Anise*

LENTIL AND VEGETABLE STEW

SERVES FOUR

This is a delicious vegetarian dish. You do not have to stick totally to these vegetables, but try to keep the balance of root to leaf vegetables for flavour and texture.

INGREDIENTS

$1/2$ lb (225 g) parsnips
$1/2$ lb (225 g) leeks
$1/2$ lb (225 g) carrots
$1/2$ lb (225 g) onions
$1/2$ lb (225 g) potatoes
$1/2$ lb (225 g) green cabbage
$1/2$ lb (225 g) red lentils
1 pt (600 ml) water
2 tablespoons olive oil
$1/2$ teaspoon Alpine Salt
Black pepper

METHOD

Peel the parsnips, carrots and potatoes. Trim, split and wash the leeks carefully, making sure you get out all the grit. Peel the onions and wash the cabbage. Cut all the vegetables into walnut-sized chunks. Put the oil in a saucepan and add the onions, leeks and lentils when the oil is hot. Turn in the oil until they are coated. Pour in the water and simmer for 20 minutes until the lentils are on their way to becoming a purée. Then add the other vegetables and the seasoning, and simmer for about 10–15 minutes until the lentils have completely puréed and the vegetables are suspended in a wonderful, savoury sauce. This is best served in bowls with lots of crusty granary or wholemeal bread. Not only is this delicious, but you also feel virtuous eating it!

COURGETTES PROVENÇALE

SERVES FOUR

There are at least three virtues to this dish: it has some of the taste of sunshine and the south about it, it is the quickest vegetable dish you have ever made, and courgettes are now available all year.

INGREDIENTS

$1/2$ lb (225 g) courgettes
1 tablespoon olive oil
1 teaspoon garlic salt
1 tablespoon tomato purée

METHOD

Wash, top and tail the courgettes and slice them into rounds about a quarter of an inch (5 mm) thick. Heat a solid saucepan with a lid over a high heat. When it is really hot, add the oil and immediately add the courgettes. Put on the lid and give the saucepan a good shake. Hold the lid down! After 45 seconds, take off the lid, and add the garlic salt and tomato purée. Put the lid back on, shake the pan vigorously again, cook for 45 seconds – and serve. That is it. The courgettes are hot and crisp, and the tomato and garlic have formed a coating over them. This dish is really that quick, that effortless and that delicious!

PASTA WITH MUSHROOM SAUCE

SERVES FOUR

Supermarkets have recently introduced a range of new products, many of which are Italian oriented. For this recipe, ordinary hard pasta is fine, but also available is a huge variety of fresh pasta: *capelletti* (little hats), *agnolotti* (sort of flat envelopes) and, of course, *ravioli*. If you are cooking this as a vegetarian dish, look for the pasta stuffed with spinach or mushrooms and ricotta cheese. For the sauce, look for the new varieties of mushrooms – oyster mushrooms, shitake, or chestnut mushrooms. They cost more but the return in terms of texture and flavour is high.

INGREDIENTS

For the sauce

1 onion

4 oz (110 g) mushrooms

1 tablespoon olive oil

14 oz (400 g) chopped Italian tomatoes with herbs

2 tablespoons tomato purée

1 clove garlic

Extra basil and oregano – optional

Alpine Salt and pepper

For the pasta

Sufficient fresh, stuffed pasta of your choice for four!

METHOD

Put on to boil a large saucepan of salted water. Finely chop the onion and garlic. Heat the olive oil in a frying pan, fry the onions and garlic until softened, then add the tomatoes, and season generously. You can add a little extra basil and oregano at this point, even if you are using herbed tomatoes. Let it simmer for about 10 minutes. Meanwhile, put the fresh, stuffed pasta into the boiling, salted water. Bring back to the boil and cook for 5 minutes. Take the pan off the heat, put on the lid and leave for 10 minutes when the pasta will be perfectly cooked. Wash but do not peel the mushrooms, slice them finely and add to the tomato sauce for another 5 minutes' cooking. Drain the pasta, put it in a big, warmed dish and pour over the sauce. Serve with grated Parmesan. If you eat this in the garden on a sunny day, it will take you straight to Tuscany without having to buy the air ticket.

PASTA PRIMAVERA
SERVES FOUR

This is a lovely, light dish in the style of northern Italy, where they use a lot of green vegetables with pasta. It looks particularly pretty if you use the *tricolore* pasta spirals which come in red, green and gold, though I have to say they taste the same!

INGREDIENTS

¹/₂ lb (225 g) pasta spirals
¹/₂ lb (225 g) each broccoli, young courgettes and fresh peas or string beans
5 fl oz (150 ml) fromage frais
Alpine Salt and freshly ground black pepper
1 oz (25 g) butter
4 tablespoons freshly grated Parmesan if available – it makes all the difference!

METHOD

Start by cooking the pasta. I discovered this method for hard pasta on the back of a pasta packet in Clapham in 1974 and have used it ever since. Put a large saucepan of water on to boil and add a pinch of salt and a little olive oil. When boiling, put the pasta in and leave to boil for 3 minutes. Take it off the heat, put the lid on, and leave for 7 minutes. At the end of that time it will be perfectly cooked, not sticky but *al dente*. While the pasta is cooking, prepare the vegetables. In a frying pan with a lid, put half an inch (1 cm) of water. Cut the broccoli into small florets and shell the peas or trim the beans. Trim the ends off the courgettes, cut them lengthways into 4, then slice into batons about 2 inches (5 cm) long. Bring the pan of water to the boil, add the butter and put in the broccoli and the peas or beans, put the lid on, turn the heat up to maximum and cook for 5 minutes. Take the lid off, add a pinch of salt and the courgettes, put the lid back on and cook for another 2–3 minutes. The vegetables will be crisp and bright green. The pasta, too, should just be finishing cooking. Drain the vegetables and the pasta and, in a big bowl, mix them together. Season generously, add the fromage frais and toss gently. (If you really don't care, you can use 4 or 5 tablespoons of double cream instead!) It is wonderfully creamy and succulent, green and gold. Sprinkle freshly grated Parmesan over each serving and eat!

TOP: (from left to right) *Courgette Provençale, Pasta with Mushroom Sauce, and Pasta Primavera*
BOTTOM: *Baked Stuffed Tomatoes with Prawns* (left) *and Stuffed Peppers*

STUFFED PEPPERS

SERVES FOUR AS A MAIN COURSE, EIGHT AS A STARTER

This is a lovely summery dish, very economical and nutritious.

INGREDIENTS

4 green and 4 red peppers
1/2 lb (225 g) cooked long-grain rice
4 oz (110 g) spring onions – or ordinary onions if you prefer
1 lemon
2 oz (50 g) raisins
1/2 lb (225 g) courgettes
2–3 tablespoons olive oil
Good pinch Alpine Salt
Small handful chopped parsley

METHOD

Trim and chop the spring onions very finely or chop the ordinary onions, and trim and chop the courgettes into very small chunks. Grate the lemon rind and squeeze the lemon. Mix the lemon rind, juice, raisins, chopped onions, courgettes and oil with the rice, and stir thoroughly. Cut the peppers in half lengthways and leave in the stalk. With a sharp knife, cut round the inside to take out all the seeds and white membrane. Put a heaped amount of rice mixture into each pepper half and then lay them very carefully in a baking dish. Pour a cupful of water into the bottom of the baking dish to stop the peppers burning and sticking. (The water will evaporate during cooking.) Put the dish into a medium oven, gas mark 4 / 350°F / 180°C / 160°C fan-assisted oven, or the bottom of an Aga roasting oven for about 35–40 minutes. When they are cooked, take the peppers out, sprinkle the top with parsley and season generously – do not do this before cooking, it makes the peppers go soggy. You can serve one of these as a starter or two as a main course, hot or cold. They have a wonderful richness to them.

MEXICAN RICE

SERVES FOUR AS A SIDE DISH, TWO OR THREE AS A MAIN COURSE

This is very delicious and can be served as a side dish. It is so full of goodies, however, that it can also be eaten on its own as a main course, especially if you are vegetarian.

INGREDIENTS

½ lb (225 g) long-grain rice
1 red pepper
1 green pepper
Bunch spring onions
½ litre (20 fl oz) *passata*
½ lb (225 g) sweetcorn
½ lb (225 g) broad beans or lima beans (fresh or frozen, not dried)
A few drops chilli sauce – optional
Alpine Salt and pepper

METHOD

Measure the rice in a cup or jug for volume, then put it into a large saucepan. Clean and chop the spring onions – use both the white bits and the green bits – and the green and red peppers. Put them into the saucepan with the rice. If you are using the chilli sauce, add a few drops now. Then add twice the volume of liquid as rice – put the *passata* into the same jug you measured the rice in, then add enough water to make it twice the volume you had of rice. Pour it in, season generously with salt and pepper, and bring to the boil. Add the sweetcorn and the beans. Simmer with the lid almost on, but not quite, so a little steam escapes. Simmer for between 15 and 18 minutes, depending on how quickly the rice absorbs the liquid. Make sure it is just a simmer, not a rolling boil. What will happen is that the rice will absorb all the flavours and colours. It becomes a bright rich red, with jewel colours through it from the beans, the sweetcorn, the chopped peppers and the onions, and all the flavours will have blended marvellously. You can eat this as a dish on its own (there is a lot of protein in it from the beans) or you can eat it with grilled foods or roast meats. What is really delicious is to eat it with an avocado mashed with a little oil and lime juice. (Otherwise known as Guacamole – see page 22.)

TOP: *Mexican Rice and Guacamole*   BOTTOM: *Classic seasoning from the Alps*

Potatoes Chariadas

POTATOES CHARIADAS

SERVES FOUR

This is a potato dish from South America. Potatoes were first cultivated in the high Andes, in the area that came to be ruled by the Incas, and were all colours. This is either a vegetarian main dish or you can serve it with grilled meat or fish.

INGREDIENTS

2 lb (1 kg) potatoes
1 large onion
14-oz (400 g) tin chopped Italian tomatoes
1 tablespoon oil
1 tablespoon butter
Alpine Salt and pepper
5 fl oz (150 ml) whipping cream or fromage frais
6 oz (175 g) grated cheese – Lancashire or Cheddar

METHOD

Peel and chop the onion. Wash the potatoes and cut out any nasty bits, then boil them in their skins. Meanwhile sauté the onion in the oil and butter. When it is translucent, add the tomatoes. Cook for 3 or 4 minutes. When the potatoes are cooked, drain them and rough cut them into bits the size of walnuts. Pile them into a dish. Add the cream or fromage frais to the tomato and onion mixture, and stir. Do not let it boil if it is fromage frais, it will separate. You can boil the cream. Add the cheese, season with salt and pepper, and stir over a very low heat until the cheese just melts. Pour the mixture over the potatoes. You can then just eat it, as in South America, but I prefer to put it under a hot grill for a few moments until it crisps up a bit and bubbles on the top. It is the most warm and comforting food you can imagine!

POMMES AU DAUPHINOIS

SERVES FOUR

This is widely and, in my opinion, correctly regarded as the best potato dish in the world. Good enough to eat on its own, it is equally delicious with grills or roast meats.

INGREDIENTS

2 lb (1 kg) good firm potatoes – Pentland Squire, Cara, Désirée or King Edward
5 fl oz (150 ml) double cream
5 fl oz (150 ml) milk
1 clove garlic
1 oz (25 g) butter
Alpine Salt and pepper

METHOD

Peel the potatoes and wash and slice them lengthways, as thinly as you can. The slicing blade of a food processor is perfect for this. Take a gratin dish, about $1\frac{1}{2}$ inches (4 cm) deep, and rub round the inside with the cut garlic. Then grease it with the butter after the garlic has dried. Put in the sliced potatoes in neat layers, and add salt and pepper. Carefully pour the milk and cream over the lot, and put into a medium oven, gas mark 4 / 350°F / 180°C / 160°C fan-assisted oven, or the bottom of an Aga roasting oven for 45–50 minutes until the top is crisp and golden and the inside wonderfully creamy. Eat with sausages, grilled meat, or on its own with good bread.

BEANS SAUTÉED WITH GARLIC

SERVES FOUR

The Chinese thought of this first, but you do not have to cook an entire Chinese meal to enjoy these beans! The ones you need are the little ones like shoe laces. Sautéed with garlic they are quite pungent, very delicious and good enough to eat as a dish on their own, which is how I prefer them.

INGREDIENTS

1 lb (450 g) string beans
1 large fat clove garlic
1–2 tablespoons groundnut or sunflower oil
1 cup water
Pinch Alpine Salt and freshly ground black pepper

METHOD

Wash the beans then top and tail them. If you do this individually, it will seem like a lifetime's work. What you do is take a handful of beans, hold them vertically over a chopping board and shake them gently in your hand until the tip of each bean just touches the surface of the board. Once they are all level, lay them flat and cut off the ends. Do the same with the other end and in no time the beans will be trimmed. Heat the oil in the largest frying pan you have – the idea is to lay the beans in as near one layer as possible, rather than heaped up. Put the washed beans into the hot oil and add the finely chopped garlic. Turn the beans in the oil and garlic for 2 or 3 minutes. They will start to go bright green. Put in enough water just to cover them, about quarter of an inch (5 mm) deep, and turn up the heat to maximum. The water will boil away as the beans cook. It will only take 7 or 8 minutes. As soon as the beans start to sizzle as the water boils away, sprinkle them generously with salt and a good scrunch of black pepper, turn them and, as soon as the water has completely gone, serve them. The water has taken some of the garlic flavour and boiled it into the beans, the beans are lightly coated and glistening with oil but not greasy, and the pepper and salt just set it all off.

PETITS POIS A LA FRANÇAISE

SERVES FOUR

You really need 2 lb (1 kg) fresh peas for this, to allow for the number consumed during the podding process. It is a lovely way of cooking peas. We eat it in little bowls on its own but you could serve it with plain grilled meat or fish. You can use fresh peas, frozen *petits pois* or even mangetout. There are a number of ways to cook this dish – here are a couple.

INGREDIENTS

1 lb (450 g) shelled fresh peas, frozen peas or mangetout
1/2 lettuce heart or 1 Little Gem lettuce
6 spring onions
2 oz (50 g) butter
Alpine Salt and pepper
1/2 cup water

METHOD

Shred the lettuce heart into little ribbons with a sharp knife. Clean and shred the spring onions. Put the butter into a good solid pan with a lid – non-stick is best. Add the onions and lettuce. If using fresh peas, add them and about half a cup of water, and cook gently for about 10 minutes. If using frozen peas, let the onions and lettuce cook for 7 or 8 minutes, then add the peas and cook for a further 2 or 3 minutes. Do not add any water – there is enough in the frozen peas already. When they are cooked there should be a little sauce. Add salt and pepper to taste, and serve.

INGREDIENTS

2 lb (1 kg) fresh peas (in pods)
Bunch spring onions
1 Little Gem lettuce or the heart of a full-size lettuce
8 fl oz (225 ml) double cream
1 oz (25 g) butter
Pinch chopped fresh mint
Alpine Salt and pepper

METHOD

Put a saucepan of water with a good pinch of salt on to boil. Shell the peas and, when the water has boiled, put in the peas and cook for 5 minutes only. They will go bright green and be almost, but not completely, cooked. Drain them from the saucepan and put to one side. Trim, wash and chop the lettuce and spring onions – both the green and the white bits. Into the same saucepan (now quite empty) put the knob of butter. As soon as it has melted, add the spring onions and lettuce. Turn them for a couple of minutes, then add the peas. Turn the heat down to the absolute minimum, put on the lid and let them simmer for about 3–4 minutes. Turn up the heat, add the double cream, balance the seasoning, then, (though the French do not do this) add a pinch of fresh mint. I think it adds the most delicious freshness. Bring the cream to the boil, but do not let it cook for more than 1 minute more. The peas will still be firm and the sauce quite delicious. Serve it with lots of French bread to soak up the marvellous juices.

Petits Pois à la Française

SPINACH PIE
SERVES FOUR

The pastry for this is made with potatoes. It is easy to prepare and, unlike most quiches which tend to have a dry texture to them, it is beautifully moist because the potatoes play such a significant part.

INGREDIENTS

For the pastry

1 lb (450 g) potatoes

2 oz (50 g) self-raising flour

2 oz (50 g) butter

1 egg

Pinch Alpine Salt

For the filling

1½ lb (700 g) fresh spinach or ½ lb (225 g) frozen leaf spinach

2 eggs

4 tablespoons double cream

Pinch each Alpine Salt and grated nutmeg

METHOD

Boil the potatoes then mash them with the butter. While they are still warm, slowly sift in the flour. Mash it in. Do not do this in a food processor, it will turn to glue. Add a good pinch of salt and then the egg. Work them in thoroughly and you will produce a very dense but quite workable pastry. Either roll out the pastry or – as I do – just press the pastry with your hands into the base and sides of an 8-inch (20 cm) pie or flan dish; very tactile and very easy! It will make a rim about half an inch (1 cm) thick. For the filling, beat the 2 remaining eggs until they are smooth and add the cream. If the spinach is fresh, wash it thoroughly and put into boiling water for about a minute until it has cooked down. Drain it thoroughly. If the spinach is frozen, heat gently to de-frost it, then drain. Mix the spinach into the egg and cream mixture, add a good pinch of salt and a good pinch of nutmeg, pour it on to the pastry, and bake in a reasonably hot oven, gas mark 5 / 375°F / 190°C / 170°C fan-assisted oven, or the middle of an Aga roasting oven for about 30–35 minutes, depending on how deep your pie dish is. The deeper it is the longer it will take. When ready, the spinach filling will have set and risen slightly, and will have a slightly golden top to it. Slice it to find a wonderful, succulent, creamy spinach filling on really moist and delicious potato pastry.

ONION QUICHE
SERVES FOUR

There is a saying in America that real men do not eat quiche. Well, real men both make and eat them! Onion Quiche is particularly good for hearty appetites out of doors. Making pastry is fun but, unless you make it all the time, it is much easier to buy it from supermarkets.

INGREDIENTS

¹/₂ lb (225 g) rich short-crust pastry
1 lb (450 g) Spanish onions
1 tablespoon butter
2 whole eggs and 1 extra egg yolk
7 fl oz (210 ml) full-fat milk
Pinch grated nutmeg
Alpine Salt and pepper

METHOD

Grease an 8-inch (20 cm) flan tin, preferably one with a loose base, and line with the pastry. I don't roll out the pastry, I just knuckle it into the flan tin. If there is a little hole, just pull some pastry across. And before you disapprove, it was Elizabeth David herself who taught me to do it! Peel and finely slice the onions, and lightly fry them in the butter for about 10–15 minutes until they are pale gold. Do not let them brown, but they need to be cooked. Fill the pastry case with the onions, then in a bowl beat together everything else – that is, the 2 whole eggs and egg yolk, the milk, pinch of nutmeg, the salt and pepper – and pour it on to the onions through a sieve to catch all the stringy bits of egg. Bake it in a hot oven, gas mark 7 / 425°F / 220°C / 190°C fan-assisted oven, or the top of an Aga roasting oven for approximately 25 minutes. Turn the oven down a little for the last 5 minutes until the top is completely set and just golden brown. I eat it warm, when it is still slightly risen – the onions are almost sweet from the frying, and the egg mixture and slight taste of nutmeg are just wonderful.

CHAMP
SERVES FOUR

This is just the best mashed potato. It comes from Ireland, where it is eaten as a meal by itself. You can, however, eat it with grilled chops or sausages – something simple.

INGREDIENTS

2 lb (1 kg) good potatoes – Pentland Squires, King Edwards or Caras

4–5 tablespoons milk

Bunch spring onions and a handful fresh parsley

1½–2 oz (40–50 g) butter

½ teaspoon grated nutmeg

Pinch Alpine Salt and freshly ground black pepper

METHOD

Wash and trim the spring onions and parsley, and chop finely. Wash but do not peel the potatoes. Some recipes say you should, but I prefer not to; the skins are full of fibre and vitamins and I like the taste and texture. Make sure they are roughly the same size and boil until tender. In the saucepan mash the potatoes very thoroughly, add the milk and chopped spring onions and parsley while the potatoes are still hot, and mix thoroughly. Put the lid on and leave for a couple of minutes. The heat from the potatoes mellows the flavour of the spring onions. Add the nutmeg, season generously with salt and pepper, and stir again. In Ireland, you heap a pile of champ on to each plate – rather like a volcano with a dent in the middle. Put a knob of butter to melt into the dent and count the calories! Here you can do the same, or stir the butter into the potato and eat it with plain-grilled meat or fish. Either way, it is just wonderful!

COURGETTE PÂTÉ
SERVES FOUR

Courgettes make the most delicious vegetarian pâté and, if you make this in the summer when courgettes are cheap, it is very economical too.

INGREDIENTS

1 lb (450 g) courgettes

2 oz (50 g) butter

2 eggs

2 spring onions – optional

Pinch marjoram, fresh or freeze-dried

Pinch thyme, fresh or freeze-dried

Alpine Salt and black pepper

METHOD

Wash and trim the courgettes and cut into slices about half an inch (1 cm) thick. Melt half the butter in a pan and cook the courgettes in it gently for about 10 minutes until they are just soft but not pulpy. Put them into a food processor – but leave them for a moment. Into the pan put the remaining butter and break in the eggs and soft scramble them. If you like the flavour, you can add a couple of trimmed and chopped spring onions and mix them in. Add the eggs to the courgettes in the food processor, together with the herbs and a generous seasoning of salt and pepper, otherwise this can be a very bland dish. Then whizz it all, scrape the sides and whizz again. You wind up with a beautiful gold and green flecked purée. At the moment it is flopsy but put it into a soufflé dish, chill for 2 hours, and the butter and eggs set. It remains soft so you can cut it with a spoon but makes a spreadable, delicious vegetarian pâté – perfect for a summer lunch.

STIR-TOSSED CABBAGE

SERVES FOUR

This is a wonderful way of cooking cabbage in almost no time at all. It is so good that everyone eats it in huge quantities even if they have never eaten cabbage in their lives before!

INGREDIENTS

1$\frac{1}{2}$ lb (700 g) good crisp green cabbage, washed and trimmed
1$\frac{1}{2}$ oz (40 g) butter
$\frac{1}{2}$ teaspoon Alpine Salt and freshly ground black pepper
1 cup water

METHOD

This needs a very large saucepan with a close-fitting lid. Place the saucepan over a fierce heat and put in the water and butter. While the butter is melting, cut the cabbage into ribbons half an inch to one inch (1–2.5 cm) wide. When the water has boiled and the butter melted, put all the cabbage into the saucepan, add the salt, put on the lid and give it a vigorous shake.

Hold on to the lid! Put it back on the maximum heat for 1 minute. The effect is to steam-cook the cabbage, preserving the vitamins. Take off the lid and grind a good scrunch of black pepper into it. Put the lid back on and give the saucepan another vigorous shake. Place it back on the heat for another 45 seconds, and that is it. I just tip the whole lot into a bowl as the buttery juices are lovely too. The butter has coated the whole of the cabbage, which is hot, crisp, bright green and delicious.

CARROTS COOKED WITH STAR ANISE

SERVES FOUR

Star anise is the Chinese version of aniseed. You can find this spice in most supermarkets or speciality shops. The shells are star-shaped, about 1 inch (2.5 cm) across, and when you crack them open the seeds have that wonderful rich new conker chestnut colour. I use organic carrots for this dish; their natural sweetness is unequalled by the other kind!

INGREDIENTS

1$\frac{1}{2}$ lb (700 g) carrots
3–4 star anise seeds
Pinch sugar (or large pinch if you are not using organic carrots)
1 oz (25 g) butter
Good pinch Alpine Salt

METHOD

Peel and trim the carrots and cut them into rounds about the thickness of a pound coin. Put them into a wide, solid pan, which will hold the carrots in not more than 2 or 3 layers. Add the aniseeds, which you can leave in the shell, the sugar, salt, butter and enough water just to cover everything. Cook over a fierce heat, turning a couple of times, until the water boils away and the carrots have just started to sizzle. At that moment the carrots will be done. The flavour of the star anise will have penetrated the carrots and produced a slightly exotic taste which blends with the sweetness and the salt from the flavourings. The butter and sugar coats them so you get these spiced, glazed carrots which make the most delicious addition to almost anything.

SALADS

CAESAR SALAD
SERVES FOUR

This comes from America, the great capital of meal salads – salads which are more substantial than something you eat with steak or chops. In spite of its name, it is reputed to have been invented in Florida for a gentleman down from Chicago for the sake of his health in the 1920s. He, in fact, was known as Little Caesar and the state of his health was probably more to do with the local cops than doctors! Whether or not this is true, it is a splendid salad with crispness, sharpness, crunch and flavour.

INGREDIENTS

1 Cos or 2 Little Gem lettuces
2 slices of bread, for croutons
2 tablespoons oil
1 clove garlic, finely chopped
2 tablespoons grated Parmesan

For the dressing
1 egg
2 tablespoons fresh lemon juice
4 tablespoons olive oil
1 teaspoon sugar
$\frac{1}{2}$ teaspoon Alpine Salt

METHOD

In a saucepan, put some water on to boil the egg. Cut the bread into cubes about half an inch (1 cm) across and fry them in the oil with the peeled and finely-chopped garlic until golden. Remove the croutons, but leave the garlic behind unless you want to be overwhelmed by it! Wash, dry and tear the lettuce into postcard-sized pieces, put it into a salad bowl and sprinkle the croutons on top. Then place the egg into the boiling water and boil for exactly 1 minute. Take the egg out of the water with a spoon, crack it and scoop all of it out – it will be lightly coddled. Mix it with the olive oil, lemon juice, sugar and salt. You can put it in a blender and whizz it, or simply whisk it with a hand whisk. Pour the dressing on just before you are ready to serve, toss the salad well, and sprinkle the grated Parmesan over the top.

SALADE NIÇOISE
SERVES FOUR

This is the classic Mediterranean salad, originally from the countryside around Nice and perfect for lunch on a hot day. Use the best ingredients – crisp green lettuce, sweet tomatoes, Jersey Royal potatoes – and serve in the prettiest salad bowl you have!

INGREDIENTS

1 Webbs Wonder or Cos lettuce
1/2 lb (225 g) tomatoes – preferably cherry type
1/2 lb (225 g) new potatoes
1/2 lb (225 g) stringless green beans – the thin ones
4 eggs, hard-boiled
1/2 lb (225 g) tuna fish, tinned
2 oz (50 g) anchovies, tinned
Black olives – optional
For the dressing
4 tablespoons olive oil
2 tablespoons freshly squeezed lemon juice
Pinch Alpine Salt
Pinch sugar

METHOD

Boil the potatoes until just tender and the trimmed stringless beans until they are slightly crunchy – *al dente*. Plunge the beans into cold water to cool. Wash and dry the lettuce and tear it into quite small pieces. Spread out the lettuce in a large bowl or one of those lovely white china ones – this salad looks so pretty that it is worth making in a super container. Wash the tomatoes, halve them if they are the baby ones, or cut into quarters if they are bigger, and put them in a ring round the edge. Shell the hard-boiled eggs, cut them into quarters and put them in a ring. Then put the beans in a ring, followed by a ring of potatoes. You may have to cut these in half unless they are really small. You now have a series of wonderful concentric circles. Drain the tuna, break it up a bit, and pile into the middle. Separate the anchovies and arrange in a decorative pattern over the salad – a lattice design looks very effective. Sprinkle over a few black olives, if you are using them. Pour the oil from the anchovies over the whole thing. Mix the dressing ingredients and whisk until thick. Pour over the salad and serve immediately with hot crusty French bread. Don't toss this salad, you'll spoil the look of it!

RICE SALAD

SERVES FOUR

This is the perfect salad for a picnic. Most salads just do not travel; they wilt within the hour. This one is robust and also tastes just as nice if you eat it at home.

INGREDIENTS

½ lb (225 g) cooked long-grain rice
Bunch spring onions
2 sticks celery
6 oz (175 g) exotic frozen mixed vegetables – the kind with peppers, sweetcorn and so on
For the dressing
1 tablespoon lemon juice
2 tablespoons tomato sauce (i.e. ketchup!)
1 dessertspoon sugar
1 dessertspoon soy sauce
3 tablespoons oil
Good pinch Alpine Salt

METHOD

Clean and finely chop the spring onions. Trim and slice the celery into very thin half-moons. Put the frozen vegetables into a pan of boiling water, let it come back to the boil and then drain immediately. Do not be tempted to cook them longer. Pour cold water over them to stop them cooking further and to cool them quickly. Drain them well again, then mix the vegetables with the onions, celery and rice. In a separate bowl, mix the dressing ingredients – the lemon juice, tomato sauce, soy sauce, sugar, salt and oil. Give it a thorough stir. If it will not amalgamate, add a couple of tablespoons of cold water to turn it into a smooth sauce. Put the dressing into the rice mixture and turn it thoroughly. It tints the rice the palest rose pink. After an hour in the fridge, the flavours will have developed and turned into the most lovely piquant dressing for a firm and crunchy salad.

Salads (from left to right)*: Spinach Salad, Rice Salad* (top)*, Salade Niçoise* (bottom)*, Caesar Salad, and Salad with Walnuts and Walnut Oil*

SPINACH SALAD
SERVES FOUR

This is an American idea. Americans often take it one step further and eat it 'wilted', that is, they put a hot dressing on it so the spinach begins to go soft. I am not very fond of that, to be honest, and much prefer using baby spinach which is now available ready-washed in packets from most supermarkets. It is not cheap, but one packet makes a lot of salad. The measurements I have given here are for a main course salad. To serve as a starter, simply use half the quantities, or double the people.

INGREDIENTS

1 lb (450 g) baby spinach
2 slices wholemeal bread (for croutons)
A little oil for frying
1 teaspoon mixed herbs, or thyme and marjoram
For the honey and sesame dressing
1 tablespoon runny honey
1 tablespoon lemon juice
3 tablespoons vegetable oil (as tasteless as possible, not olive!)
Good pinch Alpine Salt
1 clove garlic
1 tablespoon sesame seeds

METHOD

If you have not managed to buy the ready-washed spinach, wash it well – it can be gritty. Shake it dry and put it into a big salad bowl. If the leaves are on the large side, tear them in half. If you have bought baby spinach, open the packet and pop the leaves in the bowl! Cut the bread into small cubes and fry them in just a little oil, turning occasionally until they go a light golden colour. Sprinkle the herbs over them. Put the honey, lemon juice, vegetable oil, salt, clove of garlic and sesame seeds into a liquidiser or food processor and whizz until frothy and well blended. Just before serving the salad, pour on the dressing, sprinkle with croutons, and then all you need for a perfect summer lunch is some crusty bread and butter, with a little fruit and cheese to follow.

SALADE ELANA

SERVES FOUR

This is my favourite salad, a combination of two great summer traditions – cucumber and strawberries. It is properly named Salade Helena, but I call it Salade Elana after the girl whose birthday I once made it for!

INGREDIENTS

1 long but not fat cucumber
1/2 lb (225 g) ripe strawberries
Alpine Salt

For the dressing

2 tablespoons each olive oil and sunflower oil
Juice of 1 lemon
Good pinch Alpine Salt
1/2 teaspoon sugar

METHOD

Wash and trim the cucumber and slice very thinly. Arrange the cucumber on a plate in concentric circles. Sprinkle with salt and leave for 10 minutes while you are doing everything else. Slice the strawberries not quite so thinly, then make the dressing. Whisk together the lemon juice, salt and sugar, beat in the olive oil, then the sunflower oil. Pour the liquid off the cucumber – the salt will have drawn out some of the juices – and arrange the strawberries in more rings on top of the cucumber. It looks beautiful with the pale green of the cucumber and bright red of the strawberries. Pour the dressing over and serve immediately. If you can, make this on a chilled plate, and do not let it sit about – it will not improve with waiting! This goes perfectly with poached salmon and new potatoes.

SALAD WITH WALNUTS AND WALNUT OIL

SERVES FOUR

Walnut oil has a wonderful, fresh, nutty flavour, though keep the bottle in the fridge once opened. Two or three different kinds and colours of leaf go best in this salad.

INGREDIENTS

6 tablespoons walnut oil
2 oz (50 g) shelled walnuts
1 lemon
1 teaspoon sugar
1/2 teaspoon Alpine Salt
Lettuce, frisée and radiccio – or any combination of leaves you happen to like

METHOD

Tear the salad leaves into smallish pieces. Never cut lettuce – all the liquid will drain out and the leaves will be soft and floppy. When you tear the leaves, you crush the veins closed and the liquid stays inside. Wash the pieces thoroughly, put in a clean tea-towel to dry – whirl it round your head if you like! – until all the water has gone, then put the leaves into a big bowl. In a separate bowl, put the lemon juice, sugar and salt and whisk thoroughly together. Add the walnut oil and whisk until it has emulsified and is smooth and cloudy. Just before you are ready to eat, pour the dressing on to the leaves and toss thoroughly. Sprinkle the walnuts which you have lightly crushed in your hand over the top and you have a marvellous crunch, a bitter-sweet dressing and a fantastic nutty flavour. Serve as a first course with French bread and butter, or as a light summer lunch with fruit and cheese to follow.

Salade Elana

Greek Salad

GREEK SALAD

SERVES FOUR

This is one of my favourite salads. Fundamentally it is tomatoes with an oniony dressing, black olives and feta cheese. You can now buy all the ingredients in supermarkets here, including those big Mediterranean tomatoes. Apart from the dressing, which has a touch of the Crafty about it, this is pretty well what you would find on Skiathos!

INGREDIENTS

2 lb (1 kg) very ripe Mediterranean tomatoes

6 oz (175 g) feta cheese

2 oz (50 g) black olives

For the dressing

Bunch spring onions

Handful fresh parsley

4 fl oz (120 ml) olive oil

6 fl oz (180 ml) non-olive oil

Juice of 1 lemon

2 tablespoons red wine vinegar

$1/2$ teaspoon sugar

$1/2$ teaspoon Alpine Salt

METHOD

Wash the tomatoes and slice them thickly downwards. Layer them in overlapping rows on (ideally) a big white china plate – the contrasting colours look fantastic! Cut the feta cheese into half-inch (1 cm) cubes, sprinkle over the salad, and sprinkle the black olives on top. Wash, trim and chop the spring onions into small pieces, and wash and chop the parsley. Put the spring onions, parsley, salt and sugar, oil, lemon juice and wine vinegar into a liquidiser and give it a quick whizz until you have a lovely flecked green dressing. Traditionally in Greece they slice onions and put them on the salad, but I think that can be a bit pungent! Pour the dressing over the tomatoes, feta cheese and olives, leave it if you can for about 20 minutes, then serve it with that Greek bread with sesame seeds baked into the crust – or good granary bread.

HOME-MADE MAYONNAISE

SERVES FOUR

This is very easy to make, very light and very nice. It lasts for up to 3 weeks in the fridge, but it is made with raw egg so, if you are elderly or pregnant, it is better not to have it, or to give it to very young children. Provided the egg is fresh and comes from a reputable source, the rest of you should be all right.

INGREDIENTS

1 large egg, at room temperature
8 tablespoons salad oil – sunflower, safflower, etc.
2–3 tablespoons olive oil
$^1/_2$ teaspoon Alpine Salt
$^1/_2$ teaspoon caster sugar
1 tablespoon lemon juice

METHOD

Put the egg, olive oil, salt, sugar and lemon juice into a blender or food processor. Place the lid on firmly and process for a few seconds. Then switch the machine back on and pour the salad oil in through the hole in the lid in a thin stream. About half way through you will notice a change in tone as the mixture suddenly thickens and begins to emulsify. Continue pouring until all the oil is in. Just occasionally, the mayonnaise can separate. If it does, add a tablespoon of ice-cold water to the food processor, switch it on and the mixture will emulsify. When it is made, pour into a bowl or screw-top jar if you want to keep it for any length of time.

FLORIDA FRUIT PLATE

SERVES TWO

This is a straight steal from the most expensive hotel on Miami Beach, which is where I first had it. It is an illustration of the way the Americans approach dieting – though I have to say this is not the way that I would do it! What it is, though, is a marvellous plate of assorted fruit and salad vegetables with cottage cheese.

INGREDIENTS

1 avocado

½ bunch radishes

1 apple

1 pear

1 ripe peach

Small punnet of strawberries – about 4 oz (110 g)

Bunch white seedless grapes

Small carton soured cream – or low fat plain yoghurt if you are serious about the diet!

Small carton cottage cheese

Alpine Salt and pepper

Lemon juice

2 sprigs mint

METHOD

Peel the avocado by drawing a line through the skin at half-inch (1 cm) intervals with a sharp knife and you will find the ribbons of skin peel off very easily. Split the avocado in half, take the stone out, and put each peeled side down on a chopping board. Cut through it lengthways in half-inch (1 cm) slices but do not cut through at the butt end. Put the avocado on the serving plate, press down gently on it with the heel of your hand and it will slide into a fan. (Sprinkle the avocado with a little lemon juice to stop it turning brown. Do the same to all the cut and peeled fruits as you prepare them.) Wash and core the apple and pear, and slice into neat shapes. Slice radishes into neat shapes. Halve the peach, take the stone out and slice. Arrange the fruit and vegetables around the avocado halves on a plate. Decorate with the grapes and the sprigs of mint.
Mix together the cottage cheese and the soured cream or plain yoghurt, and season generously. Spoon it either over the avocado as a dressing, or in decorative blobs around the plate, and put the strawberries on top of the decorative blobs. It looks wonderful, is quite delicious and, if you use yoghurt rather than cream, and are seriously dieting, this will only do you good!

TOP: *Florida Fruit Plate*   BOTTOM: *Italian Fish Salad*

ITALIAN FISH SALAD

SERVES FOUR

This is a main meal salad, based on pasta and fish. It is marvellous for a hot day, perhaps eaten in the garden with the scent of jasmine wafting on the summer breeze!

INGREDIENTS

½ lb (225 g) shell pasta
12 oz (350 g) fish – haddock, cod or even salmon
4 oz (110 g) peeled and cooked prawns
2 oz (50 g) mayonnaise
2 oz (50 g) fromage frais
1 lemon
1 head of fennel
1 bay leaf
2 peppercorns
Squeeze of lemon juice
Alpine Salt

METHOD

Put a saucepan of water with a good pinch of salt in it on to boil. Cook the pasta for 3 minutes. Take it off the heat, put the lid on and leave it for 7 minutes, by which time it will be perfectly cooked. To save energy, you can put the fish into a steamer or colander over the pasta and steam it, so when the lid goes on it will cook nicely. If you prefer, you can poach the fish in water separately with a bay leaf, a squeeze of lemon juice and a couple of pepper corns. It will need to simmer for just 5 or 6 minutes. Drain the fish and the pasta and let them cool. Cut the lemon in half and squeeze half on to the pasta and half on to the fish as they are cooling. When they are quite cool, put the pasta in a neat shape around the edge of an oval dish. Trim and chop the fennel finely, flake the fish and mix the two together so you have a crunchy texture mixed with the softness of the fish. Blend together the mayonnaise and the fromage frais, and mix in with the fish and fennel. Pile the mixture into the middle of the pasta, and decorate it with the prawns round the border of the pasta, so you have a greeny-white (or pink, if you used salmon) centre, the pale creamy gold of the pasta and the pink of the prawns. It will keep in the fridge for a good couple of hours. Eat it on its own, with perhaps just a good chunk of that wonderful Italian dolcelatte cheese, and peaches and pears for pud!

WARM POTATO SALAD

SERVES FOUR

The best potatoes to use for this are new Jersey Royals, or any salad variety of potato – Fir Apple Pink, Kipfler or Charlotte. They all stay firm when cooked and do not disintegrate into mush, which is crucial! Americans eat potato salad with frankfurters, coleslaw, grilled meat and so on. But this is also very nice on its own, or eaten with Florentine Fennel Spoons and grated carrot. It is also quite delicious if you prefer to eat it cold.

INGREDIENTS

1 lb (450 g) new potatoes
Bunch spring onions
1 oz (25 g) fresh parsley
4 tablespoons mayonnaise – home-made is ideal
2 tablespoons fromage frais or Greek yoghurt
Good pinch Alpine Salt and pepper
1 teaspoon French mustard
1 tablespoon lemon juice or cider vinegar

METHOD

Scrub but do not peel the potatoes. Cut them into even-sized pieces and put them into a pan of cold water with a big pinch of salt. Bring to the boil and cook until the potatoes are just tender. It should take between 8 and 10 minutes, but depends on the size of the potatoes. When they are cooked, drain them and cut them into pieces roughly the size of dice. Trim and chop the spring onions and do the same with the parsley. Mix the fromage frais, mayonnaise, mustard and pepper together and, when the potatoes have stopped steaming, sprinkle them with salt and a tablespoon of lemon juice or cider vinegar. While the potatoes are still hot, they absorb that sharp edge and saltiness. Toss the potatoes in the mayonnaise and fromage frais mixture, add the spring onion and parsley and turn it all together. If you have never eaten hot potato salad, you are in for a treat! You can, of course, let it cool. It is delicious, light and, because of the combination of parsley, spring onions and firm potatoes, has a marvellous fresh texture.

$\mathscr{P}$UDDINGS

APRICOT MERINGUE

SERVES FOUR

Summer is the perfect time to make this as the shops are full of fresh, ripe apricots. This is a 19th-century recipe, originally called apricot soufflé. Don't be put off – it is definitely meringue, very easy to make, and has a lovely combination of textures.

INGREDIENTS

1 lb (450 g) apricots
$^1/_2$ lb (225 g) sponge cake or sponge fingers
5 oz (150 g) caster sugar
5 fl oz (150 ml) double cream
5 fl oz (150 ml) milk
3 egg whites

METHOD

Wash the apricots, halve them and take out the stones. Cut them in half again and put them with 2 oz (50 g) – that is 2 tablespoons – of the caster sugar into a non-stick pan. Add a couple of spoonfuls of water, and stew the apricots very gently until they are lightly puréed. Break the sponge cake into bits and put in the bottom of a baking dish – preferably a pretty one so you can serve the meringue straight from it – and pour the double cream and milk over the sponge cake. Spoon the apricots over the top of that. Whisk the egg whites until they are thick and fold into them the remaining caster sugar, spoonful by spoonful, until it turns into a soft meringue. Spoon it over the apricots and put it in a low oven, gas mark 3 / 325°F / 170°C / 150°C fan-assisted oven. If you have an Aga, this cooks beautifully in the top of the low oven. Leave it for about an hour until the meringue has set. Depending on your oven it will either be a pale gold or still really quite white. The whole thing is hot through, the cream has melted into the cake, the apricots are beautifully smooth and the meringue topping has crunch!

Apricot Meringue (left) *and Rice Pudding with a Difference*

RICE PUDDING WITH A DIFFERENCE

SERVES FOUR

This is simply the best rice pudding I have ever eaten. It is made with ground rice which is an 18th-century tradition. Ground rice, or little bits of flaked rice, was what was left in the bottom of the big sacks of imported rice. Merchants sold it off cheaply – it was not substantial enough for savoury dishes or pilau, but the ease with which it melted into cooking liquid made it great for puddings.

INGREDIENTS

2 oz (50 g) ground rice
1 pt (600 ml) milk – full-cream or Channel Island milk is best, though you can use semi-skimmed
4 eggs, separated
4 oz (110 g) caster sugar
4 oz (110 g) butter
1 oz (25 g) slivered almonds
2 oz (50 g) mixed peel – the sort you put in Christmas cake
$\frac{1}{2}$ teaspoon nutmeg

METHOD

In a saucepan stir or whisk the rice into the cold milk until smooth. Add the sugar and bring gently to the boil, giving it a stir. It will thicken and the sugar will melt. Simmer for a minute, add the butter, and stir it in until it has melted. Allow to cool. Mix the 4 egg yolks into the mixture, then beat 3 of the whites until firm and you can turn the bowl upside down. Fold into the mixture and add the almonds. Into the bottom of a buttered, oven-proof basin or soufflé dish (or for a dinner party – 4 individual soufflé dishes) put the mixed peel. Then pour this lovely almondy mixture into the dish or dishes and place in a *bain marie* – a roasting tin with an inch (2.5 cm) of hot water in it. Sprinkle the nutmeg on top. Put it into a medium oven, gas mark 4 / 350°F / 180°C / 160°C fan-assisted oven, or the bottom of a Aga roasting oven for 35–40 minutes. Make sure it does not burn; if this looks likely, put some butter paper over the top. The pudding needs to cook until it is firm through. When cooked, spoon it out, making sure everyone gets the almonds, the scrumptious rice-and-butter mixture and the marvellous high-flavoured candied peel. Serve fairly quickly before it sinks. It is one of the most wonderful puddings you have ever eaten!

BAKED CUSTARD
SERVES FOUR

This is wonderful when made with Channel Islands milk. It makes *crème brûlée* fade into insignificance!

INGREDIENTS

¹/₂ pint (300 ml) Channel Islands milk
2 large eggs
1 oz (25 g) caster sugar
¹/₂ teaspoon vanilla essence
¹/₂ teaspoon grated nutmeg

METHOD

Warm the milk in a non-stick saucepan. Thoroughly beat the eggs in a bowl until they are a lemony sort of colour. They will be frothy rather than thick. Add the sugar and vanilla essence. Mix into the milk, then pour the whole mixture through a fine sieve – this gets all the stringy bits out – into a 1-pint (600 ml) soufflé or custard dish that you can put in the oven. Sprinkle with the nutmeg, place the dish in a baking tray with an inch (2.5 cm) of hot water in it to make a *bain marie* and bake in a low oven, Gas mark 2 / 300°F / 150°C / 140°C fan-assisted oven. If you have an Aga, this cooks beautifully in the top of the simmering oven, though it will take a little longer than in conventional ovens. Cook for about 40–45 minutes until the top is golden and the whole thing set to a jelly. Take it out and let it cool, then chill it. As it chills, it sets, until after a couple of hours it is quite firm and you can cut it cleanly. I just put it in a bowl and eat it. If you have a few lemon thin biscuits to go with it, you will have a small but exquisite moment!

BAKED BANANAS WITH LIME
SERVES FOUR

This is one of the simplest of all fruit puddings to make. It never ceases to delight, both in appearance and flavour. It is a slightly tropical pudding, but both the main ingredients are easily available.

INGREDIENTS

4 large bananas – gold, not brown
4 heaped teaspoons demerara or soft brown sugar
1 lime
Double cream to taste!

METHOD

Heat the oven to gas mark 5 / 375°F / 190°C / 170°C fan-assisted oven, or the top of an Aga roasting oven. Put the unpeeled bananas into the hot oven on a baking tray for about 20–25 minutes. The skins will go completely black. Do not panic. This is the intention. When they are quite black, put each one on to a serving plate (they look best of all on pure white plates) and then slit open the skin of the bananas like a canoe, so you can see the flesh nestling in the skin. Sprinkle with the brown sugar which is there to add crunch rather than more sweetness, then cut the lime into quarters and squeeze the juice on to the sugar on each banana, so on to all that sweetness and crunchiness goes a wonderful cutting, sharp, citrus edge. Pour the cream inside the skin, on top of everything else. Eat it with a teaspoon, but be warned. This in our house is known as DHP*. And it is!

*Damn Hot Pudding

BLACKCURRANT FOOL
SERVES FOUR

This is a short fat pudding, best served in long thin glasses! It is very, very rich. Unless you freeze blackcurrants (which I do, just for this), this is a pudding which can really only be made in the two or three summer weeks when blackcurrants are plentiful. It is not *quite* as wicked as it might be: instead of using half a pint (300 ml) of double cream, it uses a quarter pint (150 ml) of double cream and the same of yoghurt. This reduces the fat content considerably, while leaving the same wonderful taste and texture.

INGREDIENTS

1 lb (450 g) blackcurrants
Up to 6 oz (175 g) caster sugar
5 fl oz (150 ml) double cream
5 fl oz (150 ml) plain yoghurt
Ginger or lemon thin biscuits – optional

METHOD

The easiest way to de-stalk black- (and red-) currants is to hold the end of the stalk and run a fork down it so the currants just pop off. Put the de-stalked and washed blackcurrants into a non-stick pan, and taste them to see how much of the sugar you need. Add the sugar and just a little water so they do not stick to the bottom of the pan. Bring them very gently to the boil and stir them. Cook for about 10–15 minutes until they are pulped and the sugar is completely dissolved. You can then push the blackcurrant purée through a sieve. This takes a minute or two, but it is worth doing to get rid of the pips. Whip the cream until it is really thick and then add the yoghurt a spoonful at a time, and rewhip. The cream will absorb the yoghurt but will remain thick and creamy, even though the fat content is no longer what it might have been! When the blackcurrant purée is cool, stir it gently into the cream mixture so as much air remains as possible. If it is marbled, that is fine – I prefer that to a completely blended mixture. I love the deep purple colours streaking through the white. Pour it into glasses rather than bowls, so you make the most of the lovely colour effect, and chill it in the fridge for about 2 hours. A word of warning – it is fiercely rich, so if you think you may want more, you do not! You can serve it with a couple of ginger or lemon thin biscuits.

From left to right: Blackcurrant Fool, Apple Snow and Apricot Amber

APPLE SNOW
SERVES FOUR

This is a delightful pudding with a delightful name. It is light, easy to make and wonderfully refreshing – as well as being a variation on the standard ways of cooking apples.

INGREDIENTS

1 lb (450 g) Bramley cooking apples, peeled and cored
1 egg
5 fl oz (150 ml) plain yoghurt
2 oz (50 g) caster sugar
Pinch Alpine Salt

METHOD

Cut the apples into chunks and put them into a saucepan. Add the sugar and just a little water, and cook very gently until the apples are flopsy like snow. They will take about 15 minutes. Separate the egg and beat the white until really thick. (You do not need the yolk.) Add a pinch of salt and the white will get even thicker. It is stiff enough when it passes the upside-down test. When the apples have cooled, fold in the egg white gently, then the yoghurt. Spoon into individual dishes, and put in the fridge for an hour or so until set.

APRICOT AMBER
SERVES FOUR

This is a lovely, easy golden pudding; warm, scrumptilious and covered in slivered almonds. Dried apricots are high in fibre and very good for you. If you can, buy the unsulphured kind – they are not such a bright orange as the sulphured ones but have fewer additives.

INGREDIENTS

1/2 lb (225 g) dried apricots
6 oz (175 g) fromage frais with 8% fat
2 oz (50 g) slivered almonds

METHOD

Soak the apricots in water, water with a dash of lemon juice or cold Earl Grey tea. That really is delicious. The tea adds a lovely, deep citrusy flavour. When the apricots have soaked for 3 or 4 hours, cook them gently in the liquid until they are soft. It will take between 10 and 15 minutes. Allow them to cool a little, then put them into a food processor or liquidiser, add enough liquid to allow them to move a little, and process for a few seconds until they are puréed. Put them into a bowl, mix in the fromage frais and pour into individual bowls or wine glasses to let the amber colour glow through. Let it set in the fridge for 2 to 3 hours, then scatter with slivered almonds. You can dot it with a bit more fromage frais or even double cream, but the nicest thing is to eat it as it is – with the wonderful contrast of the sweet succulence of the apricots and the crispness of the almonds.

PANCAKES
SERVES FOUR

Basic pancakes are dead easy to make. You can make them with plain white flour, or substitute 1 tablespoon of the plain with 1 tablespoon wholemeal. That adds a lovely texture, particularly if you are eating these as savoury pancakes. (Do not make the whole thing with wholemeal flour – you will end up with shoe leather!) You also have a choice as to what liquid to use: the French use orange juice for sweet pancakes, beer for savoury ones, or just water.

INGREDIENTS

½ lb (225 g) plain flour
1 egg
½ pt (300 ml) liquid
1 tablespoon oil
Pinch Alpine Salt

METHOD

Put all the ingredients into a food mixer, liquidiser or basin and whizz or beat until blended and lump free. Let the batter stand, if you can, for 20–30 minutes. Heat a large, solid, non-stick frying pan, pour in a little oil, swirl it round then get rid of it. Remember, the pan is very hot! Also remember the first pancake never works, so if it falls to pieces don't despair. Pour in enough mixture, about a tablespoon, to make a puddle in the middle of the pan and tilt the pan so it runs round the edges. The mixture should just cover the base of the pan, not slosh about. When it bubbles, put a spatula underneath to turn it over, let it cook for another 1–1½ minutes, turn it on to a plate, put some greaseproof paper on top, and repeat until you have a stack. Every 2 or 3 pancakes, you will need to regrease the pan.

Fillings

You can serve the pancakes with all sorts of lovely fillings: Lemon juice and sugar; apricot jam and slivered almonds; creamed spinach mixed into a cheese sauce; in layers as a cake, with a layer of fromage frais and a layer of exotic fruit or honey and nuts. My favourite is a savoury pancake cake – layers of spinach and pancakes with a cheese sauce over it, and cooked in a medium oven for half an hour. To serve, you just slice it into wedges like a cake.

PEACH MELBA

SERVES FOUR

This is one of those legendary desserts that is rarely made properly. It really does need to be made with fresh peaches and fresh raspberries – tinned or frozen will not do. It is a wonderful, grand dessert when done properly – poached peach on vanilla ice-cream surrounded by a delicious raspberry coulis.

INGREDIENTS

2 peaches
1 tablespoon granulated sugar
1 clove
1 cinnamon stick
$^{1}/_{2}$ lb (225 g) raspberries
2 oz (50 g) caster sugar
The best real cream vanilla ice-cream you can find

METHOD

Dip the peaches into a pan of boiling water for no longer than 30 seconds. Be careful – it is really hot! Drain them and, before they get cold, skin them – the skin will just slip off. Cut the peaches in half and remove the stone. Pour nearly all the boiling water away, leaving just an inch (2.5 cm) in the bottom of the pan. Add the granulated sugar, the clove and cinnamon stick. Bring it back to the boil and put the half peaches into it. Simmer them for 5 to 6 minutes, until the peaches just start to go translucent. Do not overcook – you will end up with peach jam. Take the peaches out, let them cool and do not throw away the syrup in the pan. Take the raspberries and the caster sugar, and either mash them very thoroughly with a fork or briefly whizz them in a food processor or liquidiser. Strain them through a sieve to get the seeds out. Stir a little of the cold peach syrup into the raspberry juice so you get just the thickness of double cream. This is best served on individual dishes which you have chilled first so the ice-cream does not immediately start to melt. When you are ready to serve, and not before, put a dollop of ice-cream on to each chilled dish. Put half a peach round side up on to the ice-cream, pour a quarter of the wonderful raspberry syrup around each peach and eat it very quickly!

Peach Melba

HONEY AND WALNUT YOGHURT

SERVES FOUR

This is incredibly simple and perfect for when the weather is really hot. It is very pretty, and lovely and refreshing. The best yoghurt for this is Greek yoghurt – creamy and almost concentrated because it has been strained, or you can use a wholemilk yoghurt. If you are a purist, look for the marvellous dark brown Hymettos honey from Greece. It has a flavour of thyme in it. The combination of the richness of the honey, the sharpness of the yoghurt and the crunchiness of the walnuts is just lovely!

INGREDIENTS

1³/₄ pt (1 litre) yoghurt
4–5 tablespoons runny honey
4 oz (110 g) shelled walnuts, crushed

METHOD

Put the yoghurt in a big bowl and beat it a bit so it is smooth. It will change texture slightly as you beat it, becoming a little more liquid. Stir the honey into it – you may need to warm it very slightly first if it is a bit thick – so the yoghurt becomes marbled with the honey. Take half the walnuts and stir those in as well. Pour the mixture into wine glasses and put in the fridge to set. It will not become hard, just nicely firm. Just before you serve it, sprinkle the remaining walnuts over the top.

TO MAKE YOUR OWN YOGHURT

INGREDIENTS

1 small carton plain live yoghurt
1 pt (600 ml) milk

METHOD

Bring the milk to the boil, then let it cool until you can just test it with your finger. Stir 1 tablespoon of fresh yoghurt into it. Stir it around, pour into a bowl, then set it aside for 6 hours.
That's it!

CINNAMON PEARS

SERVES FOUR

In Europe we tend to bake pears with wine and spirits. In America the tradition is to bake fruit with spices. This is a wonderful shiny, golden pudding, with the most delectable aroma!

INGREDIENTS

4 large pears, not too ripe
2 tablespoons honey
1 teaspoon ground cinnamon
1 cup water

METHOD

Peel and core the pears, leaving the stalks on. Put them into a baking dish which just holds them, and pour over the honey. Sprinkle them with the cinnamon and pour the water around them. Bake in a medium oven, gas mark 4 / 350°F / 180°C / 160°C fan-assisted oven, or the middle of an Aga roasting oven for about 45 minutes to an hour, turning them once or twice. The idea is not to have them swimming in liquid but for each pear to be coated in a wonderful, golden glaze. You can serve them hot or cold – with or without cream!

SPICED APPLE TURNOVERS

SERVES FOUR

These are very special and grand spiced apple turnovers. Serve them hot with fromage frais or crème fraîche for a dinner party, or cold at a picnic. The simple addition of a touch of cornflour keeps the apple filling where it should be – inside the pastry!

INGREDIENTS

$^1/_2$ lb (225 g) puff pastry – the supermarket kinds are excellent
1–1$^1/_2$ lb (450–700 g) cooking apples
1 dessertspoon cornflour
2 oz (50 g) caster sugar
$^1/_2$ teaspoon cloves
$^1/_2$ teaspoon cinnamon

METHOD

Peel and chop the apples into marble-sized pieces and put them into a bowl. Mix in the sugar, the spices and the cornflour until the apples are completely coated. Cut the pastry into 4 equal pieces and roll each one out to a square the same size. With the back of a knife, mark a diagonal line down the middle of each one. Put a quarter of the apple mixture on one side of the line and fold (or turn!) the pastry over. Dampen the edges and press them firmly together so each turnover is quite sealed. Cut a slot in the top, brush the pastry with milk or a little egg if you like your pastry golden. Bake in a hot oven, gas mark 7 / 425°F / 210°C / 190°C fan-assisted oven, or the top of an Aga roasting oven for approximately 35 minutes. These are wonderful hot or cold – crisp, golden, puff pastry and melting spicy apple.

MANGO FOOL

SERVES FOUR

This is a marvellous, exotic sweet which you can serve after anything that has a bit of spice in it, such as a curry. You can use fresh mangoes but they are expensive and not that easy to peel. What I recommend is a tin of Alphonse mangoes – this is not the person who packed them, but the variety of mango!

INGREDIENTS

10–12 oz (275–350 g) tin of mangoes or 1 lb (450 g) fresh mangoes
5 fl oz (150 ml) double cream
5 fl oz (150 ml) plain low fat yoghurt
1 tablespoon chopped stem ginger

METHOD

Drain the tinned mangoes and discard the syrup or, if you are using fresh ones, scoop the flesh out of the skin. Put the flesh into a liquidiser or food processor and give it a quick whizz. In a separate bowl whisk the cream until really thick, then add, a tablespoon at a time, the plain yoghurt. Amazingly, it whips into the cream but the cream does not lose its bulk – it stays like whipped cream but the fat content is cut by half. It tastes like the very expensive *crème fraîche*. Then stir the mango into the whipped cream and yoghurt. You can either stir it in completely or leave it, as I do, just a little marbled – a swirl of bright golden orange mango against the pale cream. Pour it into wine glasses and sprinkle the chopped ginger on top. (If you don't have any ginger, just put a slice of mango on top.) Place in the fridge for a couple of hours where it will set quite firmly like a mousse. It is just delicious – I wish I had some now!

LEMON CREAM

SERVES FOUR

This is a wonderfully indulgent pudding made almost entirely of pure double cream!

INGREDIENTS

16 fl oz (480 ml) double cream
4 oz (110 g) caster sugar
Grated rind and juice of a large lemon
2 egg yolks

METHOD

Heat the cream in a non-stick saucepan. Add the lemon rind and the sugar and heat until it dissolves. Bring the mixture to the boil, then let it cool slightly. Add the beaten egg yolks and simmer very gently until it just begins to thicken. If your saucepan is very solid, the heat from the base alone may be enough to thicken the mixture. Whatever you do, do not let it boil again or you will have lemon scrambled egg. Once it is the right consistency, let it cool until you can just put your finger in, then stir in the lemon juice. Stir 2 or 3 times as the mixture cools, otherwise the lemon juice may cause the whole thing to separate. Pour into tall champagne glasses and chill for a couple of hours before serving. It sets to a pale gold colour. The tiny flecks of lemon rind add a little texture and the taste is really scrumptious. Serve it with thin lemon crunchy biscuits and prepare yourselves for the perfect indulgence!

Mango Fool

CLAFOUTIS
SERVES FOUR

This is a thick, wonderful pancake from the south-west of France, traditionally made with fresh – and only fresh – big, black cherries. Here you have a difficult choice. Do you remove the stones or not? My own view is to warn people, and let them get on with it, but if you have nothing else to do for the afternoon, you can stone them! This pancake is so good you can make it in the winter with apples in what is really a Welsh version of it.

INGREDIENTS

5 eggs	5 oz (150 g) plain flour
5 oz (150 g) icing sugar	1 tablespoon oil

For the fresh cherry clafoutis	*For the Welsh apple clafoutis*
1 lb (450 g) black cherries	1 lb (450 g) cooking apples
2 oz (50 g) caster sugar with ½ teaspoon ground allspice mixed in	2oz (50 g) caster sugar with 1 teaspoon cinnamon mixed in

METHOD

You can do this either by hand or in a food processor. By hand break the eggs into a nice big bowl and whisk them. Add a tablespoon of flour and a tablespoon of icing sugar, and whisk it in. Repeat until all of each are used up and you have a nice thick creamy batter. Add the tablespoon of oil and stir it in. If you are using a food processor, put in all the ingredients except the oil and whizz until a thick batter has formed. Add the oil and stir it in. Lightly grease with butter a long gratin dish or baking dish, at least 1½ inches (4 cm) deep and at least a foot (30 cm) long, and pour in the batter.

For the fresh cherry clafoutis
Put the washed cherries on top of the batter and sprinkle on the caster sugar with allspice.

For the Welsh apple clafoutis
Peel, core and cut the apples into walnut-sized pieces and mix with the cinnamon and sugar. Put the sugared apples on the batter.

Place the dish in a medium oven for about an hour at gas mark 4 / 350°F / 180°C / 160°C fan-assisted oven, or the bottom of an Aga roasting oven. The pancake rises around the fruit. You have a lovely, crunchy, spicy fruit centre in a wonderful golden pancake. Serve with cream or fromage frais.

MELON AND MANGO FRUIT SALAD
SERVES FOUR

This is perfect for early summer when the shops are full of fresh, ripe mangoes, and also of the very small, sweet round melons with crinkly yellow skins. Add strawberries and you have a wonderfully refreshing pudding which looks good too!

INGREDIENTS

1 small melon
1 mango
½ lb (225 g) strawberries
1 glass fresh orange juice
A little freshly ground black pepper

METHOD

Hull the strawberries – take the green bits off – cut them in half and grind a light sprinkling of black pepper over them. They should be in the pepper for about half an hour. Cut the mango each side of the stone and criss-cross the flesh with a knife so it comes out as mango cubes. Cut the melon in half, take out the seeds and scoop out the flesh either with a teaspoon or with a melon-baller, if you have one. Put the mango and the melon into a bowl with enough orange juice to keep the fruit moist. Just before you serve it, and not before, drain the strawberries of any juice that may have run out and stir them into the melon and mango. Do not be tempted to add anything else, it will taste like mush. What you have is a contrast in textures and flavours and colours. The pepper does not taste of pepper, it almost magically brings out the flavour of the strawberries. This looks lovely served in wine glasses.

SCHLAFFSANGER AND STRAWBERRIES
SERVES FOUR

I first tasted this when I was just 16, in a farmhouse in what was then West Germany, quite near the border with East Germany. I could not believe it. It was late July and in Britain we had only just started to have cream again in real quantities after the end of food rationing in the early 1950s. Schlaffsanger is made with Quark, a German version of fromage frais. The original, farmhouse version was made with pure double cream only!

INGREDIENTS

1 lb (450 g) strawberries
8 fl oz (240 ml) whipping cream – or double cream if you don't care!
½ lb (225 g) Quark or low fat fromage frais
2 oz (50 g) sugar

METHOD

Wash the strawberries and hull them (take the green bits out). Put half into a bowl and crush them with a fork. Whip the cream until it is really thick, then stir into it the Quark or fromage frais and the sugar. Then mix in the crushed strawberries and stir so it is pink but still slightly marbled, with a taste of strawberries and slightly sour cream (it is obligatory to taste this as you make it!). Then slice the rest of the strawberries thickly and mix into the crushed strawberry cream. Save just a few for decoration. Pile it into bowls, or into one biggish one, preferably plain white china, and decorate the top with the remaining strawberries. There is nothing more to say!

Melon and Mango Fruit Salad (left) *and Raspberry Fool*

Schlaffsanger and Strawberries

RASPBERRY FOOL

SERVES FOUR

I do not know to this day, and no one has ever been able to tell me, why these things are called fools. It is the old English name for a fruit purée mixed with a creamy substance – custard or cream. This is a lovely delicate one and takes just a few minutes to make from a standing start. When you buy the raspberries, always check that the underneath ones have not gone a bit squashy, which they have this small tendency to do!

INGREDIENTS

½ lb (225 g) fresh raspberries
2 oz (50 g) caster sugar
5 fl oz (150 ml) double cream – 1 small carton
5 fl oz (150 ml) plain yoghurt
A few fresh mint leaves

METHOD

Crush the raspberries with a stainless steel or silver fork in a china or glass bowl. Mix them with the sugar and put them on one side for 10 minutes. The sugar on the raspberries will draw out juice and bright colour. Beat the double cream until it is thick, then, tablespoon by tablespoon, beat the yoghurt into it. The yoghurt will not thin it down; if you beat it each time you put in a dollop of yoghurt, it will bulk back up again. It allows you to have twice the amount of cream, as it were, with only half the amount of fat. Swirl the raspberry and sugar mixture into the cream and yoghurt – do not mix it so thoroughly that it looks like pink yoghurt, swirl it in so that it is marbled. It looks beautiful. Pour it into glasses so you can see the marbled effect, decorate each one with a sprig of mint and put to set in the fridge for 1–2 hours. You can leave it for up to 12 hours without any deterioration. You get this marvellous colour with lovely flavours – the richness of raspberries, the slight sharpness of the yoghurt, the unctuousness of the cream, and the delicate freshness of the green mint.

CHOCOLATE AMARETTI MOUSSE

SERVES FOUR

If you are a slimmer, avert your eyes – this recipe is not for you. Italian amaretti biscuits, with their flavour of apricots and almonds, are crumbled into the richest of chocolate mousses. This is, by the way, made with raw eggs, so I fear it is also not for the elderly, the pregnant, very young children, or those with an immune deficiency.

INGREDIENTS

6 oz (175 g) bitter chocolate containing at least 50% cocoa solids
6 eggs
2 oz (50 g) unsalted butter
Juice and grated rind of an orange
6 little amaretti biscuits

METHOD

Put the orange juice and grated rind into a non-stick saucepan and add the chocolate which you have broken into small pieces. Melt the chocolate into the orange juice. Do not leave this and walk away – stir it occasionally and, as soon as it goes smooth and glossy, stop and remove the saucepan from the heat. Separate the eggs. Add the butter to the chocolate mixture, and allow it to melt in the existing heat. Do not add more heat. Stir it until the butter, chocolate and orange juice are all blended. Add the egg yolks and stir them in thoroughly. Whip the egg whites separately until they are so thick you can turn the bowl upside down. Then carefully, knocking as little air out of the egg whites as you can, fold the egg whites into the chocolate mixture. Then spoon it into wine glasses, or individual bowls, or into one big bowl. Stop when you are half way up, and crumble on a layer of amaretti biscuits. Spoon on the remaining mousse and crumble the rest of the biscuits on top. Put it in the fridge for a couple of hours to set. As you eat the mousse you get this wonderful creamy, chocolatey texture and then the crunchy, slightly bitter flavour of the biscuits. It is quite appallingly wonderful!

BAKED APPLE MERINGUE

SERVES FOUR

This is a rather grand way of serving baked apple, but remarkably simple, which is a comfort!

INGREDIENTS

4 large cooking apples, preferably even in shape
4 dessertspoons sultanas
4 dessertspoons brown sugar
1 teaspoon ground cinnamon
10 fl oz (300 ml) apple juice or water
1 egg white
2 tablespoons caster sugar
$1/2$ teaspoon cider vinegar

METHOD

Wipe the apples, core them, but do not cut through the base otherwise the filling will fall out. What you want is a sort of well in the middle of the apple. Mix together the sultanas, the brown sugar and the cinnamon, and use to pack the wells. Whisk together the egg white and the cider vinegar (do not, by the way, be tempted to use anything other than cider vinegar!) and, when it is stiff, add the caster sugar. Whisk in one tablespoon of the sugar, and then fold in the rest to make a small amount of meringue. Put the apples into a baking dish and pour the apple juice or water all round them. Then, on top of each apple over the top of the well where you have hidden the sultana mixture, put a tablespoon or so of the meringue. Put the apples into a medium oven, gas mark 4 / 350°F / 180°C / 160°C fan-assisted oven, or the bottom of an Aga roasting oven for 35 minutes. Watch them. The meringue will go golden and the apples should be cooked but still have shape and texture. Do not leave them in the oven until they turn to mush. Take them out and serve them with the liquid they have been cooked in as a sauce. If you thought of adding just a touch of cream as well, I would quite understand!

Baked Apple Meringue

PEACH BRÛLÉE

SERVES FOUR

This is a mixture of fruit and a light cream and works just as wonderfully with nectarines. If you are going to eat this immediately it is made, do not bother to poach the peaches. A delay of more than a couple of hours means you must cook them first, otherwise the juice just runs out of them.

INGREDIENTS

2 large peaches
4 heaped tablespoons demerara sugar
5 fl oz (150 ml) double cream
5 fl oz (150 ml) fromage frais

For poaching peaches only
A little water
1 tablespoon granulated sugar

METHOD

Light the grill and let it get really hot for 10 minutes or so while you prepare the peaches or nectarines. Whether or not you are going to poach the peaches, dip them into a pan of boiling water for 30 seconds, take them out and you will find the skins slip off effortlessly. Cut them in half, take out the stones and slice each half thinly.

To poach the peaches

Put the slices into a pan with an inch (2.5 cm) of water, add the tablespoon of granulated sugar and poach them for 5 minutes. Put half of each sliced peach (poached or unpoached) into a small heatproof bowl. For 4 people you need 4 bowls! Beat the double cream until it is thick, add the fromage frais and pour it into each bowl on top of the peach. Sprinkle the demerara sugar evenly over the top and put the bowls under the hot grill, as near to the heat as possible. Watch the sugar carefully and, as soon as it has quite melted, take the bowls out and let the brûlée set. Put them somewhere cool, but not in the fridge – they will go soggy. To eat it, you crack the sugar coating – by now a bit like a rich golden ice-rink – and spoon out the richness of the cream, the fruitiness of the peaches and the crunchy sweetness of the sugar topping!

TARTE FRANGIPANI
SERVES FOUR

This makes the most of the last of the winter pears – the long, thin Conference ones. Frangipani is a fragrant flower that grows in the Tropics and there is a scent about this pear tart that is reminiscent of that fragrance.

INGREDIENTS

4 large conference pears – not too ripe
12 oz (350 g) shortcrust pastry
2 eggs
4 oz (110 g) ground almonds
4 oz (110 g) caster sugar
1 teaspoon vanilla essence
lemon juice

METHOD

Grease an 8–10-inch (20–25 cm) flan or tart tin, preferably metal and one with a loose bottom and line with the pastry. Put it into a medium to hot oven, gas mark 5 / 375°F / 190°C / 170°C fan-assisted oven, or the bottom of an Aga roasting oven. Bake for 10–15 minutes until the pastry is pale gold and just dried out, but not fully cooked. Meanwhile peel and core the pears and cut into halves, lengthways. When the pastry is ready, take it out of the oven (leaving the oven on as the complete tart will be baked at the same temperature) and place on it the pears with the sharp ends pointing inwards, so they radiate outwards like a sunburst or the spokes of a wheel. Sprinkle with a little lemon juice to stop them going brown. In a bowl, mix together the ground almonds, caster sugar, eggs and vanilla. If it is too stiff to stir properly, add a little milk until it is just soft enough to move the spoon comfortably. Spoon the mixture all round the pears and bake the tart for 25 minutes. The frangipani mixture will spread in the heat to fill the gaps and rise golden like a mini-soufflé. It produces the most wonderful, fragrant, slightly sandy and almondy textured filling to go with the succulence of the pears. Remove from the tin and place on a plate. Serve it warm, not hot, and eat the lot – this is not a pudding to eat cold!

CAKES & BREAD

THE ULTIMATE CHOCOLATE CAKE

SERVES EIGHT

This can only be described and enjoyed as gross self-indulgence! It is unbelievably easy to make and, theoretically, improves if you keep it for up to 3 days – theoretically because no one to my knowledge has ever managed to keep one for 3 days! The method sounds deeply unlikely. All I can say is, trust me!

INGREDIENTS

6 oz (175 g) self-raising flour
4 heaped tablespoons cocoa powder
4 oz (110 g) caster sugar
1 dessertspoon black treacle
5 fl oz (150 ml) sunflower oil
5 fl oz (150 ml) milk
2 large eggs
1 heaped teaspoon baking powder

METHOD

You can either make this by hand in a large basin or let a food processor do it for you. Put every single ingredient into whichever you are using and either beat it very well with a wooden spoon, or give it a whizz until the mixture is smooth, dark brown and creamy. Pour it into two 7-inch (18 cm) greased and lined sandwich cake tins. Loose bottoms and non-stick make this even easier to do, though you should still grease and line them. Bake them for 45 minutes in a medium to low oven, gas mark 3 / 325°F / 170°C / 150°C fan-assisted oven, or the bottom of an Aga roasting oven, with a sheet of greaseproof paper over so they do not cook too fast. At the end of 45 minutes, test by pressing the top gently; if the cake comes back with a bounce, it is cooked, if it stays down, it needs another 5 minutes. Allow to cool, then turn out. You can now fill the cake with all sorts of wicked things. I suggest apricot jam in the middle and a little fromage frais on the top as a kind of frosting. It really is a delicious and ridiculously low-fat chocolate cake. You can, of course, use black cherry jam and whipped double cream and do the whole Black Forest number. I leave it to you and your bathroom scales!

Yoghurt and Orange Cake (left) *and The Ultimate Chocolate Cake*

YOGHURT AND ORANGE CAKE

SERVES FOUR

This wonderful, puddingy, cake comes from the Middle East. The semolina adds a lovely grainy texture to it.

INGREDIENTS

1 large orange
$^{1}/_{2}$ lb (225 g) fine semolina
3 eggs
4 oz (110 g) soft brown sugar
6 fl oz (180 ml) plain yoghurt
1 tablespoon white self-raising flour
1 teaspoon baking powder

METHOD

Grate the orange rind and squeeze the juice. Mix the rind and juice into the semolina, then beat the eggs together and add them to the semolina together with the sugar, the flour, the yoghurt and the baking powder. You can whizz it in a mixer or mix it in a bowl until it is smooth. Butter an 8-inch (20 cm) cake tin, pour the mixture in and put it into a hot oven, gas mark 5 / 375°F / 190°C / 170°C fan-assisted oven, or the bottom of an Aga roasting oven. Leave it for 35–40 minutes – it will rise spectacularly. Test it with a skewer. If it comes out clean, it is cooked; if not, cook for another 5 minutes. You can eat it hot, with perhaps a couple of spoonfuls of yoghurt – but the proper way to treat it is to let it cool a little, spear all over with a thin skewer and pour into it a mixture of orange juice and one tablespoon of runny honey. Leave it until it is lovely and moist and rumptious-scrumptious, then serve!

CHOCOLATE FUDGE BROWNIES

SERVES FOUR

These are an American invention – very gummy, sticky and scrumptious. They are also very easy to make.

INGREDIENTS

6 oz (175 g) butter or baking margarine
2 oz (50 g) cocoa
6 oz (175 g) soft brown sugar
2 eggs
2 oz (50 g) self-raising flour
2 oz (50 g) walnuts

METHOD

Melt about 2 oz (50 g) of the butter in a little saucepan, add the cocoa and stir. Cream together the rest of the butter with the sugar. You can use a food processor or whisk for this if you prefer. When it is fully blended, add the eggs and the flour, then beat in the melted butter and cocoa mixture. Grease and line a 7- or 8-inch (18 or 20 cm) square tin. You need to both grease and line it because these brownies are sticky! Stir the walnuts into the mixture and spoon into the tin. Bake in a medium oven, gas mark 4 / 350°F / 180°C / 160°C fan-assisted oven, or half way down an Aga roasting oven for about 35 minutes. When cooked it will have a rather spongy feel to it. Leave for 5 minutes, then cut into squares. Leave again for a few minutes. I like eating them while they are still slightly warm. You can let them get completely cold and ice them, but in my house they do not last that long!

STRAWBERRY SHORTCAKE

SERVES SIX

Strawberry shortcake is one of the great American recipes for strawberries, though why we should ever leave it to the Americans I have no idea – after all, I think we invented strawberries! This is a sandwich of almost biscuity cake, with the biggest, ripest, reddest strawberries and smooth, rich cream layered between.

INGREDIENTS

6 oz (175 g) butter or baking margarine
3 oz (75 g) caster sugar
10 oz (275 g) self-raising flour
1/2 lb (225 g) strawberries
5 fl oz (150 ml) double cream or fromage frais
Pinch Alpine Salt

METHOD

Cream the butter and the sugar until pale and fluffy. You can either do this in a bowl with a fork or use a food processor, which is quicker. Add the flour and salt and mix until very thick and stiff like a biscuit mixture. There is no egg in it, you notice, or any liquid. Smooth it into an 8-inch (20 cm) flan tin which you have greased and, when it is level, prick the surface with a fork. Bake for about 20–25 minutes in a medium oven – gas mark 4 / 350°F / 180°C / 160°C fan-assisted oven, or the bottom of an Aga roasting oven. Watch it carefully towards the end. It should be golden, it should not go brown. When cooked, tip out of the tin and let cool on a rack. Meanwhile, whip the double cream, if that is what you are indulging in, until stiff, and slice the strawberries. When the cake is cool, slit it horizontally with a sharp knife, such as a breadknife, so you have two thin cakes. Lay one cake down and on the cut side, put half the fromage frais or half the whipped cream. On top of that place about half the strawberries. Put the remaining half of cake on top of the strawberries, and on top of that put another layer of cream and the remaining strawberries. I stick them in vertically, if I can, so they decorate the cake. Leave for about 25 minutes, if you can bear to. You can put it in the fridge for a little while, but not more than an hour because after that the cake starts to soften. Serve it in slices. I have known people to pour a little single cream over the top of it, but I happen to regard that as a deeply serious self-indulgence!

Strawberry Shortcake

SIMNEL CAKE

SERVES EIGHT

Simnel cakes, eaten traditionally at Easter, are named after Lambert Simnel, one of the most interesting minor characters in English history. After the Wars of the Roses he was used by the defeated Yorkists to try to de-throne Henry VII. For a short time he was quite successful at convincing prominent Anglo-Irish lords in Ireland that he was the rightful King of England. His downfall came when the Irish invaded England and were defeated by Henry VII at a battle near Stoke in Nottinghamshire. The first Tudor King had a reputation for meanness and parsimony – for which Simnel had much to be grateful. Instead of executing him, (a clear waste of resources) Henry VII utilised him for years as a cook in his kitchens, and it was there that he created this cake, or one at least not too dissimilar!

INGREDIENTS

6 oz (175 g) plain flour
2 oz (50 g) cornflour
2 oz (50g) ground almonds
4 oz (110 g) butter or baking margarine
4 oz (110 g) caster sugar
6 fl oz (180 ml) milk
2 eggs
2 teaspoons baking powder

METHOD

You can make this in a processor or by hand. If you are making it by hand, cream the butter and the sugar together with a wooden spoon until smooth. Add the eggs, then the flour, cornflour, baking powder, ground almonds and milk, and mix it all together. If you are using a food processor, put all the ingredients in at once and give it a quick whizz. Make sure it is all thoroughly blended. Put it into a lined, greased 7- or 8-inch (18 or 20 cm) cake tin. Bake it in a medium to hot oven, gas mark 5 / 375°F / 190°C / 170°C fan-assisted oven, or the middle of an Aga roasting oven for about an hour. It will rise quite dramatically. Tip it out of the tin and let it cool. Traditionally it was covered in marzipan gilded with a little saffron water mixed into an egg yolk so it looked like a gold cake. I just mix a little caster sugar and ground almonds together with a little cream and spread it on top of the cake just before serving.

FOCACCIO

SERVES SIX

This is a very healthy Italian bread, full of olive oil. You can eat it on its own, served hot with an apéritif, with a tomato or pepper salad, or dipped into those sun-dried tomatoes or peppers in olive oil which you can now buy in jars in most supermarkets. What you should not do is eat it with butter and jam!

INGREDIENTS

1 lb (450 g) white unbleached plain flour
4 tablespoons olive oil
½ pt (300 ml) warm water
½ oz (10 g) fresh yeast – which is best for this – or ½ sachet dried yeast
Pinch sugar
1 teaspoon Alpine Salt
Rosemary or sage, fresh or dried

METHOD

To make the dough, put the yeast in a bowl with a little of the warm water and mash with a fork until it looks like mud. Add a pinch of sugar, leave it for 10 minutes and it will go frothy. Meanwhile put the rest of the water, the flour, a little of the salt and the olive oil into a large bowl. When the yeast is frothy, add that too. Knead it with your hands if you want to let off steam, or mix it in a food processor – most have a special attachment for mixing dough. Leave in the bowl in a warm place for about 30 minutes. It will double in size. Take the dough out, put it on a big board, cut in half and spread it a bit so you have two pieces the size of dinner plates. Sprinkle the rest of the salt over the top, then the rosemary or sage, and pat them into the dough. Put the loaves into a hot oven, gas mark 7/ 400°F / 200°C / 180°C fan-assisted oven, or the middle of an Aga roasting oven for approximately 20 minutes. The bread rises marginally; it is meant to be about as thick as a paperback book (about half an inch or 1 cm) and pale golden on the top. Do not let it go dark brown – it will go rock hard! You can eat it warm straight out of the oven. The combination of the rich, olive-oily dough, the crunchy salt and herbs is just lovely. It is also jolly good when it has cooled.

INDEX OF RECIPES

NUMBERS IN *ITALIC* REFER TO ILLUSTRATIONS